The Courage To Believe

An Inspirational True Story

by *King Kevin Dorival*

Published by Sky View Creative Circle

The Courage To Believe © 2012 by Kevin Dorival. All rights reserved. This book or parts thereof may not be reproduced in any form, stored in a retrieval system, or transmitted in any form or by any means, electronic, mechanical, photocopy, recording or otherwise--without prior written permission of Kevin Dorival.

Second Edition. 2015.

Editors: B. Barracks, A. Beauchamp, & J. M. Halbani (Eds.),

Cover Design: Raphael "Cano" Colon of *Boasting BiZ*

ISBN: 978-0-9855648-2-7

Library of Congress Catalog Number: 2012913786

For information on special discounts for bulk purchases or school version of this book, please contact:

Kevin Dorival at info@couragetobelievebook.com.

Visit my website: www.couragetobelievebook.com.

For Speaking, Mentoring, Book Coaching, Marketing Services, or Workshop Inquires Contact us at: Info@couragetobelievebook.com.

Mailing Address: The Courage To Believe International, P.O. Box 667136, Pompano Beach, FL. 33066

1. Biography & Autobiography: Ethnic Cultures – General.

TABLE OF CONTENTS

SPECIAL DEDICATION.......................... I
THANK YOU.. IV
INTRODUCTION.. III

One
THE ROYAL BLOOD LINE...................... 1

Two
HUMBLE BEGINNINGS............................ 11

Three
BEES CAREFUL.. 22

Four
I NOW DUB THEE....................................... 28

Five
REALITY CHECK... 36

Six
BLUE AND RED.. 44

Seven
TRACK FIELD OF DREAMS..................... 54

Eight
THE PALM BEACHES................................. 71

Nine
SARAH SMILE... 86

Ten
LOVE, PEACE AND GOOD FOOD............ 92

Eleven
GROWN MAN STATUS..........................102

Twelve
LION'S DEN..........................119

Thirteen
THE BIG TOP..........................131

Fourteen
WET FOOT – DRY FOOT..........................141

Fifteen
FOCUSED ON THE FUTURE..........................152

Sixteen
LIFE IN EXILE..........................169

Seventeen
REDEEMED..........................190

Eighteen
MATING SEASON..........................204

Nineteen
BIRTH OF AN ENTREPRENEUR..........................215

Twenty
I HAVE A DREAM..........................249

Twenty-One
A NEW LEAF..........................264

~ Special Dedication ~

December 12, 1955 – May 26, 2008

This book is dedicated to *Queen Rosette Pierre*, the most beautiful woman on this side of heaven, my Mother. The Lord favored and honored us when he handpicked you to be our mom; you are the core of our family's strength, dreams, and passion. Without your love, encouragement, and belief in me, this book would still be a dream.

A long time ago you knew that I would become a writer. That old noisy typewriter you bought me from the thrift store was a seed to this best seller. You pushed me to keep moving forward even when it seemed as if the mountains were too high. I now understand why you forced us to go to church when we didn't want to, get up every morning for school and to work hard at our education. You knew how vital those lessons would be for the future of our family. It's the very reason I am a man of my word today. We think of you a whole lot and wish that your grandkids would have received more of your love, hugs, and kisses. Your memory is fresh in the minds and hearts of many. I can never replace you or your gentle touch. The good ones are the ones that always leave early.

I miss and love you dearly.

Thank You!

I would first like to thank my Lord and Savior Jesus Christ, for blessing me with life and calling me into the Kingdom for such a time as this. It is an honor to have been chosen for the mission of encouraging the world.

To my siblings ~ life has been one great, big, wild, and quirky roller-coaster ride! *There is power in unity.* Words cannot explain my love and appreciation for each of you.

To my nieces and nephews, you are my real inspiration and motivation for wanting to leave a legacy for your children's children to glean from. The joy my heart receives from your carefree smiles is indescribable.

To my spiritual parents, Pastors Ed and Yvette Brinson, you are a great example of a marriage made in heaven between a man and a woman and true generals in *Heaven's Army*.

And finally, a great big *Thank You* to everyone that has been a blessing in my life through your kind words of encouragement, prayers, and support; you know who you are. Last but not least, a special thanks to all the *haters* who encouraged and motivated me through your negativity and criticisms.

INTRODUCTION

Sixteen was the age I first envisioned writing my autobiography. I may have just been talking smack back then and without insight of how very circuitous the ride would really be. However, determination and persistence paid off. Here I am exactly 16 years later and that vision is now a reality; you are holding a copy of my inspirational true story *"The Courage to Believe" in* your hands.

Though my early years may have been rough and rocky, unfortunately, there are always others among us whom have had more arduous beginnings. Nevertheless, I have paid my dues; my season of carrying a condom and gun for protection was replaced with carrying a daily planner and Bible for survival. *The mind is a terrible thing to waste* as the slogan goes, but thank God for second, third, and fourth chances to use my intellect and the gifts that were already loaded within me.

Society could stand to spend more time shaping up and working out our spiritual muscles. We would all be better from it. Everyone should go after their dreams without solely depending on others. However, we all need assistance somewhere along this journey we call "Life." I had to learn how to find worthy people with whom to work with since I was so used to being let down by those that I trusted. It's hard to find people of honor- a rare commodity. As a result, my experiences of being backstabbed, betrayed, and disappointed have created the person who found it hard to trust anyone. If someone had told me that I would one day create a company called *One Man Army*, Inc., I would have believed them. Being

The Courage To Believe

different - that's me, and quite proud of it! Some may say that I am too young to write an autobiography, but am I too young to receive the death penalty or to become a millionaire?

My influence to write comes from the teachers who believed in me as well as great thinkers and writers: General Toussaint L'Ouverture, Phyllis Wheatley, Fredrick Douglas, Malcolm X, Sidney Poitier and Mrs. Wyche to name a few.

My fascination with monarchies, stories of courageous individuals throughout history, and tales of wars and great battles also influenced my development. I can't say for certain whether I've worked harder than any other writer would have in order to complete this project, however, I will say that I've never before worked with such zeal as I have in completing this narrative. There is always opposition to purpose, and I refuse to give up on this project since it will inspire so many lives.

The purpose for penning this genre is to be a positive voice to inspire women and men, young and old in making right turns and good choices. My desire is that minds will be opened to embrace my trials, my tribulations, and my philosophies on life, liberty, and our shared pursuit of the "American Dream." But most importantly, everyone will walk away with a clear understanding on what it is to be a strong God-fearing person.

Many will read this as just another interesting story, while you will receive it as a tool for survival. From my perspective, the challenge lies in the fact that most of the population is attempting to build a *solid structure on shifting sand*, instead of a *solid foundation*. This leads to destruction, poverty, incarceration, and you guessed it – chaos. Though a good family home foundation is important, it is more critical that an early relationship with God is introduced in the home. Life is a journey along a narrow road and having a positive relationship early on will definitely give way to better choices being made earlier in life, in our homes, our communities, and in the world.

Nonetheless, there's good news; you are set to read about how someone dared to believe he could defeat the odds. My goal is that you will be inspired and the information you receive will release revelation, foster determination, cause transformation and ultimately, be a blessing. Thanks for supporting the mission of telling my story and yes, there will be a movie – God willing!

ONE

THE ROYAL BLOOD LINE

It's only appropriate to introduce my autobiography with the history of my family's country – Haiti. It's a country encompassing about 27,750 square kilometers – roughly the size of the state of Maryland. It occupies the western-third of the Caribbean island of Hispaniola (La Isla Española). The Dominican Republic takes up the eastern two-thirds, having a horseshoe shape on its side. Haiti has two main peninsulas located in the north and in the south; between these peninsulas is the Isle de la Gonaives.

Hundreds of years ago, the island of Haiti was originally inhabited by Indians who called their home Ayiti, "The Land of Beautiful Mountains" and it was known as the richest island in the western hemisphere. Some might find it hard to imagine that though the earthquake may have shaken the landscape of Haiti, on January 12, 2010, it did not shake the fabric of Haiti's incredibly strong people — my parent's people....my people! The island was traumatized, causing massive destruction and the death of hundreds of thousands of people and left an estimated one million homeless. Prior to the earthquake, Haiti was already considered the most impoverished island in the western hemisphere. However, in April of 2012, Haitian miners working for foreign investors made an astonishing discovery of an estimated $20 billion worth of gold, silver, and copper. Exactly how that money will be used toward the restoration of the country has not been clarified.

The Courage To Believe

The French invaded the land and brought people from western Africa including: Benin (formerly known as Dahomey), Coite I'voire, Togo, and Ghana. Researchers appear to be interested in Haiti's connection to Benin, supposedly the original home of my people, because its inhabitants practiced voodoo, daily. General Toussaint L'Ouverture, whose surname means "The Opening", led Haiti out of slavery and into freedom by victoriously defeating the French and Americans. It was an amazing feat given how strong the French army was, led by the infamous Napoleon Bonaparte, military and political leader. America was a young country itself, but France was known around the world for its military prowess. General L'Ouverture outwitted both countries playing them against each other (Rogozinski). A mythical legend has it that the Africans of the island sold their souls to the devil to win the battle while others say it was just pure luck. But the more realistic explanation is that the Haitians employed a well-executed battle plan by a talented general who won seven battles in seven days.

If you ask me, I would say it was destiny. The Africans were tired of working their fingers to the bones. "They were forced to work twenty-two hour shifts in sugar cane fields, which were the bread and butter of the French. Women had to work during the later stages of pregnancy and children were forced to begin working at the tender age of four, while the men could do nothing to prevent it." It was only a matter of time before the slaves had enough – an eruption was inevitable. France was going through a revolution in their own country and the men were spread thin. Meanwhile, a yellow fever epidemic in France wiped out half their soldiers, decimating the army.

The conditions were ripe for the Africans to give the French the boot.

This was no small victory. Eleven years before the battle of Waterloo, the slaves in Haiti handed Napoleon a humiliating defeat. Yet, there are people who make false over-simplifications and attempt to minimize both General L'Ouverture's military brilliance and the fierce resolve of the Haitian people to fight for freedom. The revolution in Haiti was the first and only successful slave revolt that led to a founding state in world history.

A few generations after the Haitian slave revolution, a beautiful woman was born in Cap-Haitian, Haiti on December 12, 1955. Rosette Pierre, the youngest of three siblings, and in my opinion, the sweetest person you'll ever meet on earth, my mother. Mom was a bit of a comedian, loved a good joke and always the center of attention. Her other two siblings, both boys; Eugene and Davlion Pierre were very close and did everything together. They fought other boys, dated the same girls, and farmed their parent's vast land. Rosette's father's land was so huge that other people sharecropped the land. They were allowed to work on his property to grow their vegetables and sell the finished goods at the market, which not only provided for them, but also added to the "bread and butter" for my family.

School, school, and more school was the focus for young Haitian children whose parents could afford it. The future of the natives without an education was very dim. In fact, families receiving an education were a very rare commodity. However, my mom was fortunate enough to receive a high school education, which opened the door for future generations in our family. Even so, my relatives, like most families on the island, were too busy scratching their heads trying to make it day by day to think about furthering their education. Furthermore, getting a good education was one thing, but finding a good job in an impoverished country was another story all together.

Education wasn't free then and it isn't free now. For about twenty to thirty dollars a semester, a struggling parent could send at least one child to school. (I wonder if the parents that had two or more children had to flip a coin to see which child would attend school). In the 1960's, everyone went to school as a child because life was easier and everybody who wanted to make money was making money. As soon as the presidency changed from Daniel Fignole to "Papa Doc" resources became scarce. Most young girls stayed home and became cave women while the young boys were allowed to go to school. This mindset was done to secure the family's legacy that fell on the backs of every male child born into a family.

Children were raised knowing that it was very important for them to go out into the world and make something of themselves in order to bring honor to the family name. One such honor customary to the culture was that children would take care of their parents once they retired. In contrast, it appears to be common practice for many American families (seemingly anxious) to put their parents in an assisted living facility. In the Haitian culture, however, no one likes to think about their parents living in a retirement home.

My maternal grandfather, Davlion Pierre, was a chief and also considered a judge in their small town of farmers. Most people in Haiti were and still are some type of farmer. As chief, his duty was to mediate situations as a neutral third party between feuding neighbors, couples, and business associates. The due process of law in Haiti was in the hands of those that the community trusted or was forced to trust. Every town had a chief like my grandfather that was unofficially appointed by the townsmen and townswomen, but authorities respected them all as if they were elected officials.

Life was simple over there as it is for most natives of the Caribbean. The stress over bills, taxes, and money was mostly non-existent simply because one didn't necessarily need money in order to survive like here in the United States. Living off the land is a custom for those who have no choice. I have only seen one picture of my grandfather, but I have heard many stories about his valor. From what I have learned people loved him for his nobility and admired him for his wit.

Now my grandfather's wife, my mother's mom, Marie Pierre, was a very interesting woman – tough, loud, and obnoxious. She met my grandfather at the marketplace in downtown O'cap which is where the majority of the business transitions took place in Cap-Haitian. When my grandparents were in their twenty's, Grandma was selling her soaps, fruits, and vegetables while my grandfather was looking for more than just groceries. Haitian women are tough because they know the game that men play ... the game all men know how to play for that matter. As a result of the game, the women have a wall the size of the "Great Wall of China" erected as a fortress to block

The Courage To Believe

out the male species. My grandmother was probably the toughest of all with her short stature, 5'4" and an understandable Napoleon complex to match. Stories have it that every day for two months my grandfather would go to the marketplace to see her, in hopes of catching her when the cart wasn't busy. This was his only way of getting any quality time to get better acquainted since he had no chance of speaking with her anywhere else. After many episodes of visiting my grandmother at the marketplace, my grandpa prevailed. Eventually they got together, married, and had three children. While my grandmother practiced voodoo, she never imposed her religion on her family — thank God.

Timothee Dorival, my father, was from the same Cap-Haitian neighborhood from which my mother was raised. He was a tall, dark-skinned, handsome man standing 6'1". He had to have some swag to get with a woman as attractive as my mother. Antonise Dorival, my father's mother, was a beautiful, light-skinned woman with a pretty smile. Charlise Xavier, Timothee's father, was a man about whom I knew very little. Timothee took my grandmother's last name, Dorival, because his father's name wasn't on the birth certificate. The reason behind that was due to his refusal to claim my father once my grandmother became pregnant. It was not until Timothee was a couple of years old that everyone kept telling Charlise that my father was the spitting image of him. It was then that he began to claim my father as his son in order to clean up his reputation in the eyes of his family and friends. Charlise was dishonoring his family name by disclaiming the child of a woman that everyone knew he once courted.

My mother and her female cousins, from my understanding, were kept under strict rule by their fathers from other boys in the "lakou" – a word that means neighborhood or village in Creole. Boys could not step to any of the girls in the family without risking a real beat down. Davlion Pierre, Jr., aka Uncle Joe and the oldest child, was my favorite uncle and was the original gangster of the family. Uncle Joe was a very serious individual, always had a gun by his side and was known for his "38 Hot" temper. Peter, his younger brother, was a womanizer and very abusive. I grew up watching both of these men beat up on their women ... something I've always adamantly opposed.

My Auntie Getty was the oldest of her generation; she was fortunate to attend school and eventually college at Omega University in Port-au Prince in pursuit of becoming a doctor. Haiti has always been a country of many trials and tribulations and because of that my aunt was unable to realize her dreams. Just one year shy of earning her medical degree, she was forced to leave Haiti due to its internal strife. Education was highly-prized in our family, but making sure that they were financially secure and safe was even more important. My aunt's departure was a matter of life or death.

Haiti wasn't the most democratic country during this era, but at least there was a semblance of order. Dr. François Duvalier, known as "Papa Doc" (April 14, 1907 – April 21, 1971), was the thirty-second president of Haiti and ruled from 1957 to 1971. In 1964, he dubbed himself "President for Life." Papa Doc ruled with an iron fist invoking fear throughout the land. He used both murder and expulsion to suppress his opponents. Estimates of those killed under his regime were as high as thirty thousand. Once he died, Jean-Claude Duvalier a.k.a. "Baby Doc", his son, took over at the age of 19 with all of his father's vices and a large taste for luxury. By February 7, 1986, he was overthrown and found refuge in France. This man plundered the country's financial resources by stealing an estimated $300 million to $800 million and absconding with it to France. (In 2007, the French government froze his accounts).

The people of Haiti, along with my family, left in droves during Papa Doc's reign. Like many Black nations throughout the world, Haiti was and is still controlled by foreign interests. As long as there was a puppet in power, someone was willing to play the role that kept money flowing into their hands with no concern for the citizens' well being. Countries like the United States and France were going to keep the puppets in power at any cost.

The island has been plagued with power-thirsty soldiers and corrupt officials since the beginning of the beautiful island's establishment. Haiti was a paradise on par with Tahiti before Europeans came and introduced elements into the environment that threw the eco-system irreparably out of balance. The island would further suffer due to trade embargos exacted as punishment for driving out the French.

The majority of my mother's family left the island during the 1970s. I have only traveled outside of the United States once, but have yet to visit the island that I have studied about with so much passion and have grown to love. While most of my family became émigrés of Haiti resettling in the U.S., my grandfather never attempted to leave his native land. He was much-admired by all and died in 1998. I've always been proud to know that someone in my family had a position of honor and prestige. I am sure, without a doubt, the confidence that runs deep within my whole family comes from my grandfather. May he always rest in peace.

TWO

HUMBLE BEGINNINGS

I was born on February 7, 1980 in my mother's apartment in Pompano Beach, Florida and was chauffeured to Broward General Hospital in Fort Lauderdale, Florida. Mom had five kids and two "baby daddies." I hate the way that sounds, but it is what it is. My little brother Rube and I shared the same father while the oldest of the bunch, J.C., had a different father. The youngest two, Kerlene and Pharo, had another father – the only man my mother ever married.

We were a distinctive bunch, each of us having unique characteristics from one another. But we had mad love for each other. All of us were skinny except for J.C.; he was always chubby and if he wasn't smiling you could be sure that he was eating. My grandma showered so much favoritism on him that it truly hurt the feelings of the rest of us. She would buy J.C. all types of toys, clothes, and shoes. He had Chuck Taylors in every style and every color imaginable — even a tropical blue pair with coconut trees on them.

Grandma would often give the rest of us this cold stare and say, "Don't y'all touch any of Boy's stuff!"

Her nickname for him was "Boy," and only the adults called him that. J.C. had to sneak around our grandma's back to let us play with his toys or his Nintendo game system.

I could never figure out why she went out of her way to let us know she loved him so much more than the rest of us. It remained a mind-boggling question until I became a man (which I will reveal in a later chapter).

"What did we ever do to you?" We often wondered. I wanted an answer from her, but I didn't dare fix my mouth to question Grandma. She possessed an audacious blend of compassion and disdain — compassion for J.C. and disdain for the rest of us.

Grandma didn't abuse us physically, her mouth did it all; however, she did punish us accordingly. She had this thick, brown, Texas leather belt with an enormous silver buckle. It had engravings of horses and cattle fire branded onto it that was set aside for the special purpose of handing out spankings. Whenever we misbehaved, she would tell us to kneel on the ground and put out our hands. That position together with the sound of the leather squeaking in her grasp let us know what was coming next. Once our hands were out she'd begin to hit us on our palms with five, high velocity smacks per hand, *pap, pap, pap, pap, pap.* You could hear the belt whistle in the air before touching our hands or rear ends. Once she was done, we would have to apologize to her or to whoever the conflict was with, usually one of our siblings. Then we would have to kiss the floor. I understand apologizing, beating our hands, but kissing the floor ... struck me as odd.

Rube, the third child, was as sneaky as a cat. Mom called him "Souris" which means mouse in Creole and French. His swiftness was a testament to his string bean body and his

The Courage To Believe

eyeglasses stereotypically matched his smarts. But his intelligence didn't prevent him from wearing glasses at a young age. I remember mom constantly telling Rube to stop sitting so close to the television, but he refused to listen. By the time he reached the fourth grade, his vision was so poor that he needed glasses. As for the rest of the family, we all have great vision genes. Rube was the only sibling that consistently earned the honor roll award every year in school.

Rube was on Grandma's better side – I was not. He had a sneaky trick he played for about as long as I can remember where he would put money on the floor and ask if it belonged to any of us. It could've been anything from a quarter up to a five dollar bill. I can't recall how this test went with my other siblings, but he always told me that I was the only one that never lied. He'd sometimes give the money to me as a reward for my honesty.

Kerlene, the fourth child and mom's only girl was cute when she was little and blossomed into a beautiful woman. She was spoiled rotten by everyone in the family – everyone, but grandma. Kerlene never had to share anything, not candy, food, or toys. She was the family princess. One time J.C. was playing with her and popped her bottom lip with the broom stick by mistake. Princess Kerlene's dad and our mom unleashed a whooping out of this world on him. I even felt the licks, but she was the family jewel and was not to be played with by any of us too rough. Okay, she was a girl, so I get the part about not being rough with her. Kerlene and I would be at odds with each other throughout our school years, but once we became adults, a strong and loving foundation was formed.

Pharo, the youngest, was the black sheep from the day he was able to talk. Being the youngest, he was able to get away with a lot of things that would've gotten the rest of us in serious trouble. His constant hyperactivity and wanting to be the center of attention caused him to be suspended from school relatively often. While in elementary school, he quickly made a name for himself as a troublemaker. Pharo's father would get a phone call at work at least once every two weeks to come and pick him up from school. His father had no problems with spanking Pharo right there in front of the principal, the students — the whole school. Back in the 90's principals were allowed to discipline children with a wooden paddle. Mr. Dudley, the principal at Park Ridge Elementary, had to spank Pharo so much that he eventually gave up. I guess he came to the conclusion that the axiom "spare the rod, spoil the child" didn't seem to work when it came to my brother. Nonetheless, Pharo was fun to be around. Once in a while he would chase us with his feces, which was pretty disgusting, but being the youngest he could do no wrong . . . not even when he would chase us with poop on a stick. As a child he was known for being the bad little boy who had a penchant for Popsicles. By the time he reached his teens, he had become a hotheaded street runner. We used to get him to do all kinds of crazy stunts. One Sunday morning before going to church he got the notion that he was Superman. He got on the living room couch and we rooted him on to jump.

"Superman...Superman...Superman...Jump, Jump, Jump!"

The Courage To Believe

We chanted, and he leaped into the air and his forehead landed on the edge of the glass table…bam! Blood was everywhere and for a few seconds he was unconscious. We called an ambulance and he was rushed to the hospital. We were so worried, but I was more concerned with mom, because she was in so much agony crying all the way to the hospital and all the way back home. Pharo had to stay there overnight and received stitches. That time away from him really affected us all. I realized then how much that little dude meant to me and to all of us. I was glad that he never ratted on us by telling anyone that we had enticed him to jump.

My earliest childhood memory is from when I was the age of three or four, at that time, my father was raising me with his current wife, Simone Dorival. He always had me dress-up like him from head to toe. I can recall having the same haircuts, shirts and pants as him. My full brother and I always called our father Timothee because he never earned the title "Daddy." He just wasn't around enough to develop that title, but at least he would come through every other full moon. Fathers earn the name Daddy just like mothers earn the name Mom or Mommy. He drove around in a flashy, black Thunderbird whenever he would come to see us or to drop off money. The visits eventually stopped once he was ordered to pay child support.

I can recall being in the frustrating situation of being caught in the tug of war going back and forth between my father and mom. My father wanted me to mimic him, while my mom wanted me to live with her, who at the time was unable to care for me financially. The time with my father was terrifying due to the fact that his wife was very abusive towards me both verbally and physically. Fear is the only word I can use to describe my feelings whenever she was in my presence. Timothee had a speech impediment that caused him to stutter often and it was passed down to me as well – just my luck. Perhaps that was how my stepmother justified hitting me every chance she got because I would stutter every sentence. She showered me with names like dumb, stupid, and idiot — the usual words intended to encourage a child. I hated my father for many years because he never stood up for me. I was his only child at the time.

I can recall an incident with her giving me a bath and banging my head against the wall.

"Kevin, stop all that crying and carrying on, dumb, stupid boy."

My father came in and heard her. "Good," I thought. "He won't let her get away with this." But when he came in he didn't do anything. I wasn't content with this behavior and remember forming a plan. I was going to eventually stand up for myself and run for freedom the first chance I got. I had to be four or five at the time because I wasn't in school yet. The opportunity to escape came on a weekend afternoon and I took advantage of it. It had to be on a weekend because Timothee would be off from his warehouse job and we would go riding in the neighborhoods while he checked out his girlfriends around town. My plan to flee was about to take place. Only God knows how my memory works because I'm a visual learner.

The Courage To Believe

My father went to a neighborhood that I recognized as my mom's friend's neighborhood.

As soon as he opened the car door to let me out, I jumped out and took off like a gazelle in the wild. My mother's friend's door just happened to be open that day and it appeared that she was bringing in clothes from the washhouse. I ran in and slammed the door! She had to have been shocked by the surprised visit. She picked me up to help me breathe since I was gasping for air. Timothee had no idea where I was and was probably surprised that I had taken off so quickly without an explanation. My mom came and got me like a guardian angel and I never returned to my father's house again. After I told her what Timothee's wife was doing to me, Mom, being the true "Mama Bear" that she was, put Simone on her hit list! Mom couldn't wait to give her a piece of her mind.

The living conditions with mom weren't the best because we were always struggling to eat and pay bills, just like the lyrics described in "Dear Mama" by the late great, Tupac Shakur:

"Shed tears with my baby sister over the years we were poorer than the other little kids. Even though we had different fathers it was the same drama when things went wrong we blamed mama....A poor single mother on welfare tell me how you did it....Dear Mama."

Mom was struggling by herself to make sure that we had food on the table and the bills were paid, but despite working two jobs, there were times when all of her efforts weren't enough. The lights and water were cut off many times, but never simultaneously. I think there should be a law preventing utility companies from shutting off lights or water where children reside.

Tupac went on in his song:

"I wish I can take the pain *away if you can make it through the night there's a brighter day, everything will be alright if you hold on. It's a struggle every day you got to roll on. And there's no way I can pay you back, but my plan is to show you that I understand."*

That part always hit home because we would cry as kids out of pure frustration wondering why our fathers didn't care about us enough to help our mom or to spend time with us. It was a miracle that a single mother could raise five children on welfare, but we relied on faith, willpower, and the love for each other. There were times when our lights were off so often that we literally had to wait for the sun to rise to see a brighter day.

There were plenty of times that we would pray over our food and eat by candlelight – a humbling experience. I still pray before every meal – no matter how small – and remember the effort that my mom made to keep us fed.

On those occasions when the water was turned off, we had a system. "Ya'll wait here. I 'ma get the bucket," J.C. instructed. The rest of us waited around the side of the house for J.C. to return with the white, plastic bucket. Once he returned we all lined up, crouched down, and crept between our house and the neighbors'.

The Courage To Believe

"Okay, I'll say 'green' if the car is gone and 'Murdock' if it's there," Rube announced. He scurried around to the neighbor's carport. "Green, Green," Rube said. We were like Navy Seals on a mission. On Rube's word and J.C.'s leading, we quietly made our way over to the neighbor's outdoor water hose and filled up our bucket. Mission accomplished – now we could take a bath.

Most likely our neighbors would have given us the water, but our pride wouldn't allow us to ask. We would be in the backyard in our underwear, one-by-one with our mother bathing us to make sure that the water was being used sparingly. It was from those experiences that I learned water is more valuable than electricity. I actually enjoyed those moments as I have always enjoyed the outdoors.

During that time, mom had three kids, all boys: J.C., Rube, and me. J.C. lived with my grandmother, while Rube, the youngest, and I stayed with our mother. We had a tight bond with our mom, even at a young age. If mom were sleeping on the floor, then we would sleep on the floor. If mom was happy, we were happy. If mom was stressed out, we were stressed. But when she was hungry, we were still full. As a great mom would, she always took care of us first.

My older brother J.C. lived with my grandmother because she felt that he was her son and the rest of us were "Rosette's kids." It was typical of her to treat her grandchildren with bias. Before J.C. was born, mom hooked up with his father in the Bahamas. While she was pregnant, J.C.'s father became very irate about the pregnancy and tried to kill my mother with a brutal attack while she was seven months pregnant. By God's grace she survived and J.C. was born healthy. Our grandmother was there through the whole ordeal and that is why J.C. was her favorite grandchild. J.C. always yearned for a relationship with his father – he's the kind of person that is warm and affectionate where anyone is concerned. Nevertheless, his father never came forward, neither in the Bahamas nor in the United States.

Like most mothers in the ghetto, whenever they were stressed out, it was taken out on their kids; especially when it was time for discipline. That's exactly what my mom did when she was stressed. If we talked back or did something that wasn't right in her eyes, whatever my mom could grab in sight she would throw at us; it didn't matter if it was a cup, radio, shoe, plate, or elephant horn. Usually there wasn't any warning not like how today's children are given ("Little Joey, I'm going to put you in time-out!") we usually went straight into a good old-fashioned whooping. One thing I know for sure, her aim was pretty good … really good. I can now laugh at those times, but it wasn't funny back then. Kids will be kids and we misbehaved a lot, but some things were blown out of proportion when it came to disciplining us. I guess you can say I was beaten a lot as a child, but she is my mom and has the right to discipline her children as she sees fit, to a certain extent, of course. Like all parents, Mom would've benefited from a child discipline course.

My mother loved us dearly and we loved her as well, but back then she was on another level sometimes with that ole' school-style spanking.

The Courage To Believe

Around the age of seven, I recall asking my mom for some crackers. "Mom, could I open up the Ritz crackers?" "Okay, but don't make a mess," she answered.

I opened up the box, took a stack of about five or six crackers and placed the box back on the table. I didn't realize that I left a bunch of broken crackers on her bedroom carpet in front of the television. Now, my little brother Rube watched TV a lot, real close up. When Mom saw the mess on the floor she flipped out. Naturally, in my five-year-old mind I felt that it could have easily been Rube who left the mess in the spot where he always sat. That was a conclusion I hoped she would come to since Rube was only four and too young for a good whooping. The trouble was that Mom felt I was the culprit because Rube didn't ask for any crackers. I was the only one.

She grabbed one of her high heels and hit me on top of my head a few times. Each word yelled was punctuated by a blow.

"Pick (swat) up (swat) behind (swat) your (swat) self (swat) (swat)!"

The stiletto heal caught me a couple of times breaking the skin. In my mind I was wishing Rube would've told her that it was him that left the mess, but he was only four and could only watch in agony. As I was picking up the bits of crackers, blood was pouring down my face onto the crackers in my hands. Mom froze for a moment in shock once reality kicked in that she had seriously injured me. She cleaned me up and apologized the next morning. I'm not sure what she was thinking or going through at the time, but my head was seriously hurting. A small gash on the top of my head was the end result. At least this incident sprung me from school for a day and I got a chance to hang out with my favorite Uncle Joe and his favorite girlfriend, Auntie Lisa. That was always fun.

THREE

BEES CAREFUL

    We had two uncles: one was cool Uncle Joe and the other was mean Uncle Eugene, but both were close with their only sister, Rosette. Uncle Joe was cool, but very hot-tempered. He unintentionally showed us the first guns and cocaine we ever saw. One could only imagine what other ghetto children witnessed in front of their parents and family. At the time, I didn't realize it, but he was cooking cocaine into crack right in front of us. What a role model! He would always come over and take us out to eat, to the movies, or to the park so that we could get some fresh air and play. Mom always kept us inside. Were it not for school or my uncle, we wouldn't have known what a playground looked like. If it wasn't about school or church, Mom wasn't trying to hear it.

    We watched our first movie at the theaters with Uncle Joe. The movie was about an Indian tribe in a snowy region that hunted whales. Uncle Joe always had an American girlfriend (Haitian men *loved* black American women back then just as we do now and vice versa). His girlfriends would cook for us after school, especially Lisa. She would cook up grilled cheese sandwiches with Kool-Aid to drink — my favorite meal as a young boy. Just the scent of the buttery, toasted bread and melted cheese would drive me crazy. We really looked forward to seeing Lisa and my uncle every day after school. Everything was an adventure hanging with them because life outside of church or school was otherwise non-existent for us. The movies sparked all of our imaginations and creativity, especially mine.

My imagination as a child was incredible and movies just made me expand my dreams and goals. Batman was my favorite because he was always alone and hated scumbags.

"I should be the black-caped crusader who lives in a mansion and owns a fleet of tricked out black Cadillacs," I thought. "By cover of darkness I would run the streets with my two trusty, black Doberman Pinchers and together we would protect the streets and the community." I suppose it was a lot for an eight-year-old child to imagine, but I loved to dream about different adventures; which were acted out when Mom was at work.

We would all make up games and go on adventures in our little apartment. "American Gladiator" was our favorite show with all the muscular gladiators pounding away at the contestants. We absolutely loved that show along with WWF (World Wrestling Federation), boxing (the Mike Tyson era) and football. Rube, J.C., Kerlene, and I even mimicked our favorite show by creating obstacle courses: a water slide, a pillow mountain, and a gladiator course. The pillow mountain was basically a pile of sofa pillows against the wall and we would fight each other within a corner of the apartment where the pillows were stacked.

Our favorite game was the water slide that consisted of one of those long, old-fashioned plastic runners that covered the floor. Haitian households used these types of mats a lot. We would pour water on the mats and run a few steps down the

The Courage To Believe

short hallway and slide on the mat. "Slide, slide, slide…" we cheered for each other.

Swish! Slosh! Bam!

"Uh, oh…ooh…"

We were having so much fun that one day we put a huge hole in the drywall. All we could do was to wait until our mom pulled up in the driveway. A view of the parking lot was in the front window. We all got on our knees with a belt, ready for her to whoop our tails. Keep in mind that all of this was done in a tiny, one-room apartment. Those were some of the best times we shared together.

As we got older, I picked up an interesting hobby. Somewhere along the line I became fascinated with bees — wasps to be exact. I was seeking fun and adventure outside of the house and away from my siblings. I would hunt down the wasps in order to rattle their peaceful nests or simply knock them down. Once the bees scattered I would take the nest and pull out their baby bees in the nest one-by-one. I must have gotten stung over 20 times. It gave me a rush to get chased by bees – I'll never know why. Eventually my brothers got in on the fun with me and we would catch the adult bees and pluck their wings. We would then place the bees into a house that we built made with wooden ice cream sticks. It got to a point where I was immune to the pain of the bee stings even though my face would swell up. Eventually, the bee hunts had to stop. All good things must come to an end, right? The only reason why the bee hunts ceased was because I got tired of fighting the other third graders for picking on me about my swollen face.

I was always a troubled young man with a flaring temper that took on its own being and earned me a reputation as a fighter in school and sometimes church. The fact of the matter was that I was just misunderstood. Young boys need a male figure in their lives to provide discipline and to teach lessons and survival skills. Mothers can only play both parents to a certain point until it's too much to handle. A woman can't teach a boy how to become a man, and a man can't teach a girl how to become a woman. We all have our roles … our various niches in society carved out by nature. Society has unfortunately distorted this quintessential principle over the years. Without both parents in the home, children are only being fed half the truth and their foundations are only half as strong as they need to be for them to navigate the tempestuous seas of this world. It certainly sheds new light on the kinds of challenges faced by an illegitimate child or even one being born to two parents in wedlock who later separate leaving only one parent in the home. Yet, God is gracious enough to make up the gap for the millions of highly successful souls who are able to succeed despite the odds.

There are so many mistakes that I would never have made if my father had been in my life. My frustration of not having a father in the household was acted out with violence towards my siblings and schoolmates. My questions of why my father didn't care about us — didn't care about me – manifested into a whirlwind of hostility. He didn't know how great his son would turn out. And to think, he could have been a part of the story. I would only have glimpses of him during my childhood.

The Courage To Believe

The mistakes I experienced due to lack of a father figure began early on. Failing kindergarten would not have happened if I had my father or another adult male figure playing a substantial role in my life. There are only two ways to fail kindergarten: 1) too many absences whether out sick or from too many suspensions; or 2) behavior problems such as constant fighting. My problem was fighting. My mom did what she could to discipline me, but she could only do so much for her little man-child. If my father had been around, he would have disciplined me as his son and I believe I would have passed kindergarten. Besides that, I would have grown up knowing the difference between aftershave and cologne.

Mom had to deal with four bad kids at the time all on her own. I can't recall what made me calm down and turn my focus to learning in school. Perhaps it was the realization that the more time she had to take away from her job to deal with me, the less money we had. That money was necessary for the purchasing of toys, clothes, and most importantly, food. After a few spankings in Jesus' name, I settled down and did what was expected of a young king. So instead of being at home or at school all of the time, we started our own "Great Awakening" and somewhere around age 11 or 12 we began going to church two to three times a week. What really fascinated us about church were the programs for kids: the field trips, the plays, and the special events (Christmas was my favorite). We always went to church together on Sundays, but we eventually started being a part of the church and its ministries. My mom made sure we were in the building. Come hell or high water, we were there! It is my deepest regret that I didn't take the piano lessons that mom signed us up for. Other than that, it was a great experience going to church because we enjoyed it!

Our mom was in the church choir and worked her way to becoming the lead singer; sometimes even singing a solo. It gave our souls peace whenever we would listen to our mother's harmonious gospel tones at home. She hummed more often than she would sing. Back in her day she was very attractive with a beautiful face, a shapely body, and the voice of an angel from heaven. At one time we attended two different churches and mom was a lead singer at both. We were always proud to watch her sing and showed our support by clapping louder and harder than anyone else, even if the other members stopped and stared.

My mother was so attractive that men were always barking at her whether it was in public or at church. I guess men will be men even in the house of the Lord. We never like the constant attention from these strange men, but we eventually got used to it. Unfortunately, we got used to a lot of other things when we were younger: constantly being broke, barely having enough food to survive, and living in apartments that were infested with rats and roaches. We were taught that God would make things better one day and we had faith that he would.

We held onto a faith that one day we would have a home with many rooms and air conditioning; we would grow up and become professionals in our chosen careers; we would have an overflow of food in our cupboards; would have more than enough money; that our mom would be able to hang up her

The Courage To Believe

uniforms from work; and that we would always be together, one way or another. Faith!

FOUR

I Now Dub Thee

As a child, my imagination was untamed. Reflecting back, one of my wildest fantasies was thinking and believing that I was royalty; in fact, a prince. This was mainly because of the V-shaped hairline on the front top part of my head; no, not a widow's peak. My V-shaped hairline faces *away* from my forehead that causes me to brush my hair in a particular way or else it would look like a patch on my head. It takes a skilled barber to know how to cut my hair. It was a nuisance then and it's a nuisance now. Nevertheless, because it was unique, I deemed my special V as royalty. In my mind, it was a unique feature and it gave me confidence despite my shaky childhood. Thinking back, this was my way to escape the reality of my world, my disappointments and all of the broken promises—my own kingdom fantasy. I was convinced that in a matter of time my African descendants would return, thereby allowing me to reclaim my destiny as "King" Kevin… yeah right!

Speaking of promises, as a little boy, I remember a situation with my father, which caused me to struggle with vows. To this day, I never make promises or accept them. I prefer to speak with action and for others to do the same—don't tell me—just show me. On one of my adolescent birthdays, my father Timothee promised to pick up my brother Rube and me, to celebrate. Excitement consumed the core of my existence because visits with Timothee was far and few between. Rube and I put on our finest clothes (as if we had many options) and

The Courage To Believe

the aftershave that was thought to be cologne. We waited, waited, and waited some more, from sun up to sun down. . My mom lovingly encouraged me to change my clothes so we could eat and watch our favorite television show, "Americas Most Wanted" together. It was our only shared form of entertainment other than trips to K-mart. No matter how she tried, mom couldn't convince me that he was not coming; I believed in him and his promises. But he never showed up or even bothered to call us until months later; sadly that day, Timothee lost my trust. I cried that night in silence and cold darkness when everyone was asleep. My heart was hardened from that experience and not just toward Timothee, but also toward everyone.

Reflecting back over the myriad of broken promises, which came through our father, it was extremely difficult to trust and believe anyone for a very long time. Whenever the words "I Promise" was spoken to me, a wall would quickly go up and my response would be "don't promise me anything!" But, as a result of Timothee's many broken promises, I grew up honoring my word, which in today's society is a rare commodity. I thank him silently for that aspect of my character. There are so many hyenas in the world, but only a few people that truly mean what they say. It is said that there is only one good man out of every ten thousand; I am determined to be one of those rare ones. As faith would have it, some of the negative experiences with my father helped develop my character for the positive. Timothee unintentionally prepared me for what to expect from most of the world… lies and deception that I would soon experience over and over again in my young life. This is one attribute that was cultivated in me and changed me from a cute cub into a roaring lion. As much as this experience affected me and caused me to grow as a man, I really wish I knew how it affected my brother Rube because he always remained gullible to our father's words. In due time, however, my heart was restored and my trust in and towards people was redeemed.

Besides the many mishaps we had as children, we also had fun learning how to be entrepreneurs without any of our father's help. At an early age, we discovered that J.C. was an artist. We transformed his talents into a successful business venture. J.C. was the family's Picasso. He was able to draw and sketch cartoons at the age of about nine years old. He came up with the idea of drawing out our names in bold, colorful cartoon letters. When other kids saw the drawings and asked if we could make them one, a light bulb sprung up in our heads. We started to market and sell the drawings between .50 cents and $2.00. Kids started wanting their names to be custom made with certain colors and themes that were cool because we were never short of orders. We would have an order list of names and the prices next to their names. All of this was possible due to the after school program we were enrolled in at the local Y.M.C.A. Rube and I would take the orders, Kerlene was the treasurer, and J.C. would make the drawings. I could honestly say that every child in the after school program that was old enough to count .50 cents bought at least one drawing. Not too bad for a young family business. Our mom was real proud of us and we would gladly try to give her the profits, but she would never take them. As a treat to ourselves, we would set up a campfire in our backyard and have roasted marshmallows. It would be nice to claim that the idea was mine, but I can't recall whose it actually was since we all loved the outdoors and animal shows on PBS and Animal Planet. While most kids were watching cartoons after school, we were watching zebras get eaten by alligators, mating seasons, or eagles and hawks soaring high in the sky. Most of the time, we were enrolled in the Y's afterschool program and spent our afternoons there.

The Y.M.C.A. was an amazing program because it allowed my mother to work more hours, which was a huge benefit for our finances. We were supervised, fed, had fun, and my mother was able to generate more money without worrying about who was watching over us. We were able to have nicer clothes and finally name brand shoes on our feet. I had my first pair of L.A. Gears™ that were red and white with red and white laces. We made some pretty good friendships in the program with some of the teachers and children that lasted well into our adult years.

One of those friendships was with my fifth grade teacher, Mrs. Wyche. As a matter of fact, my class, the class of 1992 at Park Ridge Elementary, was her first class as a teacher. And, if I'm not mistaken, her first class as a teacher. She moved down to Florida from South Carolina with her husband and son after she finished her duties in the U.S. Army. She was a tall, black woman with a fair complexion and a powerful presence. Mrs. Wyche demanded excellence in everything we did, whether it was studying, group exercises, P.E. (we loved playing kick ball), or tests.

There was a group of "Top 10" students: Sophia A., Adam B., Vanessa C., Jonathon D., Hilary E. (I had a huge crush on), Tiffany F., Kathleen G., Ebonica H., Mickey J., and Rodney P. They always received straight A's—always. Mrs. Wyche made me believe in myself and told me, "Believe and you can achieve." I never made honor roll in my younger life, but once Mrs. Wyche showed me that I could be smart too, I made the honor roll every quarter that year. I couldn't believe it! She really cared for her students and was the only teacher (I knew of) that would come to our homes to check up on us and talk to our parents. She always commented on my gold necklace that my mom gave me. She felt that it was a distraction to me and dangerous to walk around with.

One time she thought I overslept for a school trip to Bush Gardens in Tampa, FL. She got off the bus and drove to my house. The funny thing was that while she was driving toward my house, I was running through the neighborhood to the school at 5:00 a.m. because I *had* over slept and woke up in a panic. My mom didn't even know that I left, but when Mrs. Wyche came and woke her up they both realized that I was gone. I wish there were more Mrs. Wyche's in the world, especially in our underserved school systems.

Mrs. Wyche forced us to reach beyond our expected intellectual limits by challenging our mental capacity through tests, quizzes, and by asking spontaneous questions. She got us new high school desks and we did our tests on Scantron® sheets. She was breeding us for the next level ... literally placing our minds beyond limitations by making us think about skipping junior high school, going straight to high school, and then to college. My first intellectual victory came from an exam based on our country's states and capitals, as expected by

The Courage To Believe

all fifth graders. From the beginning, I knew that studying as much as possible was necessary. Up to that point in my life, this was my hardest test. Most of the students studied in groups of friends, but I opted for studying alone, as usual, and with classical music which was suggested by Mrs. Wyche. The night before the exam, I studied vigorously until my uncles and cousins came over to talk to my mom. They were eating good, talking loud, and laughing louder. I went into the boys' bedroom, closed the door, and turned off the light so they would think that I was asleep. I angled the map and used the moonlight as my lamp. The noise caused me to not be able to hear myself think and out of shear frustration, I began to cry. I was afraid, afraid of failure and a fear that I was going to disappoint my Sensei ("teacher"). I knew I couldn't tell my elders to put a sock in it or my mom would have handled me accordingly, so I cried myself to Zzzzzz instead of reviewing for the test.

A couple of days later the results were in.

"For the most part, every one of you did well on the exam, except for a couple of D's, but only one of you did excellent!" said Mrs. Wyche.

I looked at the "Top 10" saying to myself, "I wonder which one of them got the A+. Tiffany probably got it because she always gets everything right."

I knew I would get at least a B based off the amount of time I put in.

Our teacher looked me directly in the eyes and said, "Kevin Dorival, please stand up."

I stood up.

"You were the only person to get a 100% on the test-great job Kevin!" she said as she came up to me with watery eyes and gave me a hug while everyone in the class clapped.

It wasn't any of the kids from the "Top 10." It was the little Haitian kid with the gold chain and speech impediment from the projects that got a perfect 100%. It was the first time in my life I was perfect in anything. What wonders the power of words and recognition for small victories can do to inspire and encourage…setting one on a brighter path!

It was as if the heavens opened up and at that very moment I was crowned.

FIVE

REALITY CHECK

Living across the street from a high school had its many perks. Other than the occasional Deerfield High Marching Band practice, which could get a little loud, it wasn't a bad deal. I can recall every Saturday morning, my mom walking over to the high school to shop at the flea market that was held in the school's parking lot. There would be a few dozen vendors and customers that would sell, trade, and buy many desirable goods. During these outings at the flea market with my mom, I noticed how skilled she was at negotiating. Mom would negotiate every deal until the price was acceptable to her liking. As I watched my mom in action it taught me at a young age the art of negotiating. It was clearly noticeable that this skill gave her a sense of pride each time she made a deal. One day, I will continue the legacy of transferring the art of negotiating onto my own children.

We had a little Rottweiler -Labrador mixed puppy that we named Julie. She was the cutest thing and very smart. Julie was immediately drawn to my mom's gentleness and sweet smile. As with most puppies, Julie loved to play. One of her favorite games was to hide all of our socks, shoes, and slippers. Even though it was annoying at times, it was cute. I had the awesome responsibility of making sure Julie was fed each day. I was so fond of Julie that I couldn't bear to think of her being hungry or having to be left to the fate of all domesticated dogs needing to wait until their owners fed them. I skipped school once because I forgot to feed her. So I made the ten-mile hike back home to go to Julie's rescue.

Times were not always happy though. I can remember being awakened to a distraught voice saying,

"Kev, Kev, wake up! Your mom...your mom's car flipped over," shouted Robert a childhood friend that lived at the front of our housing projects.

Robert yelled again in the late night hours, "Kev, Kev, Kevin wake up man—your mom is hurt *bad*. Wake up!"

At first I thought it was all a bad dream, but there was Robert at the end of my bed, shaking my legs in the middle of the night while I slept clothed only in my underwear. Rube, Pharo, and Kerlene had already bolted out the door to where mom's car flipped over about 100 yards from our apartment at Park Ridge Court or PRC, the housing project where we lived.

My mom's cousin Teleson was in the car with her during the accident. He was escorting her home because of a stalker ex-boyfriend that wouldn't leave her alone. As kids, we were all stressed out about this guy and the police couldn't do anything at the time. His name was Estefan and he had been aggressively following our mother to work and night school. The creep was so bold-faced that he had the gall to come by the apartment, park in front of the house, and smile at us. He also had a friend who would drive his car and park in the front of our apartment while he would wait on the side of the house, hoping to catch mom opening the door to yell something at him, thinking that he was in the car. The night Robert woke us

The Courage To Believe

up from our sleep was when Estefan's jealous rage reached a boiling point. Mom was studying to become a beautician so that she could open up her own beauty salon. Our assumption of what triggered Estefan's rage on that particular night, while spying on mom, was because he saw another man pick her up from night school.

Estefan was able to use his Toyota Supreme late model coupe to hit my cousin's van head-on causing it to roll over on its side. Once the car flipped on its side, Estefan banged out the windows with a bat and broke both of my mother's arms and my uncle's arms as well. They also suffered head injuries from the car accident. Teleson was far from a chump, but being stuck in the car upside down, he was unable to defend himself or more importantly, my mother, which was his original purpose. I'm quite sure that Teleson had a gun somewhere in the car and couldn't get to it.

While my siblings and I waited at the hospital, I can remember being very angry about the situation. I wanted to cry so badly, but for some reason, I couldn't; a flaw of mine that I later developed and came to despise is not being able to cry. Looking at my beautiful mother with her arms and head wrapped up and listening to her speak with a pain filled voice wasn't easy. All my siblings and grandparents knew something was wrong with me then because I wanted to cry, but just wouldn't let the tears flow.

There are people roaming the earth with nothing, but bad intentions toward others, so I learned to be prepared at all times.

On that night, at the tender age of 13, my outlook on life suddenly changed because of that horrific ordeal. Life to me was no longer about going to school and hanging out with friends. It was about protecting my family and keeping my eyes open for sudden encounters of both good and evil. I guess you could say the attitude I took on was of a "Batman Vigilante" protector concerning my family. I was ready to crush evil people on contact. The cloak of darkness that wrapped around my soul as my mother lay bandaged up was the cape that draped across my shoulders. Thanks to that traumatic experience, the violence my mom and uncle suffered at the hands of insanity, stole my innocence before I even lost my virginity. I wasn't a child anymore. I considered myself to be a man that was going to protect my family at all costs.

Growing up in those conditions and the absence of a father, I learned quickly that the most precious gift in the world is a child. They are the present and the future. I may not have a child of my own at the moment, but I know that having one is a blessing for any parent. So much can be told about the future of a family, a church, a nation, and the world through the preparation of the children. It defines both our humanity and perpetuates it. The heart of a good parent is to give their children everything that's good, especially the things their parents couldn't afford to give them when they were children, whether monetary or spending quality time. Parents want to cocoon their children in a bubble of protection. Preserving their child's innocence is their main goal; to protect that peaceful, carefree, child-like state of mind for as long as possible. The more successful we are at this task, the more it will lessen our problems in society where children are concerned. In low income neighborhoods, from experience, it's impossible to create that peaceful state of mind in a child. Because of the environment, they are prone to think about and act out the negativity encircling them. The stability of a home matters, especially if all you have to do is look out the window and witness a cesspool of sin. These surroundings are filled with drug dealers, prostitutes, AIDS, single-mother homes, insufficiency, lack of trust in the authorities—especially the police, domestic violence, debt, etc. ... just to name a few. However, I do feel the stability of the home will give that child a better chance at not just surviving, but at succeeding despite the odds... a better chance of making good choices regardless of the negativity witnessed through the looking glass of their own abode.

Growing up in the ghetto wasn't easy, as I'm sure most people know by now, but it's an experience that can make or break an individual's spirit. I can't speak for everyone, but I picked up some noble characteristics, such as becoming a God-fearing man, a leader, ambitious, athletic, intelligent, and a survivor; all from the experiences I endured as a child reared in a single-parent home in the ghetto.

My environment and family circumstances forced me to become the man of the household by protecting, caring, and providing what I could for my mom and siblings. One of many things I'm most proud of was always making sure that my mother had something to eat every night before she went to sleep after getting home from work. I was the man of the house and my mother was determined to make all four of her boys become warrior kings. Even though I was the second oldest, I was always taking care of business since my older brother J.C. was under the guardianship of Grandma. I helped my siblings with their homework, spanked them with a belt when discipline was needed, and made sure everyone was in bed by a certain time, and all while I was still in elementary school. As children living in the ghetto, we were exposed to so much at an early age such as the stress of our parent's bills, smoking, drinking, sex, crime, police brutality, drugs, guns, the understanding of hunger, and violent deaths. People from the ghetto—the "hood" as it's often deemed, are indeed a different breed. I am of the opinion that it produces three types of people: the strong, the weak, and those that merely exist. Only the strong will survive. It's a Choice.

Before we moved into Park Ridge Court Apartments, we were living in a house with my grandmother. In the 80's, while living with grandma, we witnessed the drug business live and in Technicolor. Back then, young and old black males would sell crack and/or cocaine day and night openly, without any fear of punishment or of police harassing them. Many drug dealers would stand on the street corners waiting for a car to stop, which meant they were looking for drugs. The majority of the customers driving into our neighborhood were white and we would see a herd of black men running to these cars in hopes of being the one(s) to sell their product. Sometimes they would fight one another because they beat the other to the car. It was survival and only the strong survived the street life. The weak were swallowed up by the viciousness of the dope game.

The Courage To Believe

We saw dope fiends get beat up and stomped down to a bloody pulp on a regular basis. I have seen a couple of robberies, shoot outs, and unfortunately, even saw someone shot in the head at close range.. Surprisingly, I never get nightmares from these events, but they certainly would be enough to cause Post Traumatic Stress Syndrome in someone whose disposition was not tempered by ghetto life.

My mom and grandparents would never allow us to step foot outside the fence to play. The fence was like our plastic bubble. As long as we were within it, we could get the needed exercise, fresh air, and sunshine as well as keep us within the parameters of Mom's cocoon. We usually played touch football in the front yard that was gated. There were times when we couldn't even play outside if our mom felt that there were too many drug dealers around. All we could do was watch the other kids roam the streets like zombies while the street action became our entertainment. You never knew what was going to happen next in the ghetto.

I can recall one bright and sunny afternoon in the late 80's as if it were yesterday. Mom had just picked us all up from school—Cypress Elementary. On the way home, she stopped at a bus stop around the corner from Grandma's place to ask a woman that she knew from church if she would like a ride. The woman said, *"No, Merci,"* meaning '*no, thank you*' in Haitian Creole. Right next to her was another black woman who was very pretty and wearing an all-white nurse's uniform.

As soon as we began to drive away, a blue Chevy pulled up and a man with an afro jumped out of his car to grab the nurse. She struggled with him vigorously, but he managed to force her into his car. I guess that he was her boyfriend or husband because she said something out loud like,

"Leave me alone, I'm catching the bus!"

All of us were stunned by the way this guy hit her in the mouth. Bam! He followed it with an uppercut to the stomach. My mom stopped in the middle of the road, along with the other cars that stopped, everyone watching the whole thing go down with disgust; but nobody helped her — which was common in the hood. There were men in the area that could've done something . . . anything.

"Why doesn't someone help her," I thought.

Lord knows if I were just a little bigger I would've been swinging on him. Blood was all over her white uniform. She was fighting back though, and kept jumping out of the car but he would pull her back in every time she tried to run from him. This man was viciously hitting on her, as if she was a man that stole something from him. Eventually, the woman gave up and they drove away. That incident left us with a mental scar, but on the other hand, there was a positive lesson to be learned from the ordeal. It's the reason why I never hit women- just can't do it. This was the first of many domestic violence cases I witnessed first-hand in the black community. I despise guys like that.

SIX

BLUE AND RED

Being a Haitian a.k.a. "Zoe" wasn't as glamorous throughout the 80's and early 90's in Florida as it is now in the new millennium. We had to fight for our respect almost every day in school and in the streets. Black Americans or, as Haitians would call them, "Yanks" would pick fights with us for no apparent reason other than the fact that we were Haitian. It was very perplexing to me because we were the same color, just from different backgrounds and cultures. It was strange to experience racism from our own kind. Yanks—Black Americans were African-Americans who were born in the United States and didn't have a Caribbean background. If there was a fight, eight out of ten times it was a Haitians vs. Yanks fight. Why Yanks hated Haitians was confusing but the hatred towards Black Americans by many Haitians was understandable because we had been placed in the position of having to defend ourselves or get rolled over. Several Black Americans would jump us before, during, and after school. Some of us would run home as soon as the bell rang like a bunch of zebras would sprint from a pack of hyenas, literally.

Eventually, things started to get interesting when we turned the tables and initiated the fights instead of waiting to get hit on. My older brother, J.C, got jumped by a group of Yanks and was badly stabbed in the stomach while walking home from Pompano Beach Middle School. I don't know what caused Zoes to go crazy in other parts of the state, defending themselves and getting their respect, but in our neck of the woods we had our own situations. My brother was seriously hospitalized for a month and had to undergo surgery. After this incident, a group mainly consisting of Islanders (mostly Haitians or Bahamians) was formed that began calling themselves "Island Boyz" and repercussions were paid soon afterwards. The Island Boyz would often lean against the hallway walls and wait on small groups of Yanks to pick on. They would usually target those with a few friends unless they were in a mode for war.

"Hey Yankee, get over here."

Of course, no one walked over so they were snatched up.

"Alright boy, sing that Haitian Anthem for us one time…let's go."

"I don't know your anthem," the unsuspecting victim would say.

The Island Boyz knew the Yanks didn't know the anthem. That was all it took for the Zoes to jump on the Yanks and deliver a beating.

The transition of power was now on the Haitians side, especially, since the Haitian military joined forces with the Columbian drug lords in the cocaine business. The island was used as bridge between Columbia and Florida. Money is power and it showed in the confidence that Haitians began to have in the streets. In Miami, the Zoes over there were already on another level of gaining their respect. They were setting

The Courage To Believe

examples that Zoes were not to be messed with by putting Yanks in body bags. Haitian teenagers in Miami were using guns to get their recognition and weren't scared of shooting to kill for this respect.

That blue and red Haitian flag will always mean something special to me even though my Creole speech is a bit average, but then my English isn't exactly Pulitzer Prize winning either, I must admit. The blue symbolizes the sky; and the red represents the blood-filled battlegrounds of Haiti since the 18th century. History shows that Haitians always had to fight for respect and recognition. The school books that cared to mention how we gained our independence as the first independent black nation in 1804, tried to make it seem like it was a small piece of irrelevant history, but the truth is we had our independence since 1794. Haiti wasn't recognized by the world as a nation… the First Black Nation until 10 years later, or maybe it took the super powers of the world 10 years to realize that it wasn't a rumor. An army of Africans destroyed the mighty military of France; it actually happened.

Knowing my history would explain why I took offense when people confused me for a Jamaican or an American. I've heard that Cubans would be insulted if you referred to them as a Puerto Rican or vice versa. I've heard my share of ignorant comments like "you don't look like a Haitian," or, "you look too good to be Haitian" as if they were supposed to be compliments, but they hurt the most. The love I carry for my Haitian heritage made the so-called compliment show for what it really was—a put-down of Haitians in general. Despite receiving my fair share of comments like these, I knew most

Black Americans weren't ignorant. One such person was my next-door neighbor, Ms. Williams; she was "Ghetto with Class" and always had our back. One time these dudes were trying to beat up a friend of ours while my brothers and her son were playing football in front of our apartment complex. We stopped the game to come to his aid, but we were out-numbered 15 to 8, and we were prepared to fight with our fists up. However, we had a secret weapon ... a big secret weapon. Ms. Williams came outside with a shining, silver .45 caliber handgun.

"Y'all better take that B***S*** somewhere else," she shouted while pointing the shiny chrome gun in the air.

Those guys ran like bats out of hell. After that ordeal, a deeper respect for Ms. Williams was formed, not to mention, I already admired her for owning a beautiful champagne Cadillac Eldorado with white walls on the tires.

Despite the troubles we faced with the Black Americans, I had a crush on someone we considered as the enemy. My eyes were on a Mademoiselle my age. In the eighth grade I began courting Shai who was a young and pretty Black American. She was one of the most popular girls at Crystal Lake Middle. She stood at 5'10, 130 pounds with beautiful teeth, a winning smile, a nice dark brown complexion and with all the necessary components in all the right places for her size; a very cute southern bell all around. She and I caught a lot of slack from both sides. Shai wasn't with the negativity towards Haitians any more or less than I was toward the Black Americans.

The Courage To Believe

I was extremely shy when it came to Shai because I really wasn't a hound for girls, and also because being a virgin at the age of 15 wasn't considered cool in the ghetto. After my daily pep talk in the mirror, I gave myself my word that I would step up to the plate and talk to her. You would think that after a classmate read my palm and said that I would become this "great lover" in the future that I would be bold enough to sweep Shai off her feet. This was definitely not the case for me, or so I thought. I was happy to know that my best friend, Fat Fritz, had already leaked my interest to her. Shai was waiting on me to make my move during our lunch breaks, like a lioness under the shade ready to mate; so the longer I took the more I looked like a chump. To my surprise she had her eyes on me a lot longer than I had mine on her. She lived in my grandmother's neighborhood, which I visited every weekend to hang out with J.C, my big brother, and all the while not knowing she lived there. What a coincidence!

Our relationship was interesting because it was my first real one and the expectation was that we were supposed to follow the norm of hating each other's nationality. My first tongue kiss came from her and, in my opinion, I was better than she was. Eventually, I hit the jackpot with her and lost my virginity. Sounds cheesy, right! Especially when everyone else around my age had already been having sex since the fifth grade and I was in the eighth. I didn't even know how to put the condom on properly; I thought it was supposed to be pulled back over my balls. No wonder I was in so much pain. Virgins! She brought a confidence out of me that I never tapped into before. I knew that I wasn't an ugly boy inside or out, but I didn't realize that I had so many things going for me until Shai showed me. She pointed out that I was an ambitious, gentlemen and smart.

We broke up after she leaked private information to a cousin of hers that I was a virgin when we met and this cousin didn't like me because I was Haitian. It was embarrassing because the fellas all had a joke or two about it. As I mentioned before, it seemed as if everybody had already been sexually active since the age of 13. We argued about the rumor even though it was true. I didn't think it was anyone's business outside of our relationship, just like many other things. We ultimately broke up before the prom, but we ended up going together anyway.

Shortly after my 15th birthday, my friends and I found a gig working at a Health/Tanning Center, called "Sunglow Health Center." In the 90's and up until the mid 2000's, jobs grew on trees; if you wanted to work there were plenty available. It was a blessing because I was able to get haircuts in a timely fashion, buy myself up-to-date clothes, and chip in on the bills at home. I was balling with money in my pocket and a fine girlfriend on my arm. Having a variety of shoes and a tight dress code in the eighth grade was a big deal in my hood. My mom tried hard to make sure we had a new pair of shoes from *Payless* whenever school started and right after the Christmas break. Financially challenged mothers, like mine, sent their kids to school *looking* broke and we got picked on by other kids as a result. Kids treat other kids better when they dress nice. Once my appearance improved, more people wanted to be my friend. It was like magic overnight the way girls noticed me all of a sudden.

The Courage To Believe

The owner of Sunglow that gave me a job was Michael Finn. A middle-aged white male with a Hispanic wife, named Alex and a cute, intelligent little girl named Jessica. They were a good team and a great family. Alex managed the books and the tanning part of the store while Michael ran the health aspect of the business. They sold holistic medicine consisting of ancient and modern powdered formulas to help sick or weak individuals get better and stay healthy. Their medicine actually worked. Michael had a liquid that could cure a sore throat with a simple dip a Q-tip into it, followed by rubbing on your tonsils.

Michael was more than a boss; he was like a father figure to a few of the employees that worked for him. He knew we were from fatherless homes so he took it upon himself to teach us little lessons about life and hard work. Personally, I can't ever thank him enough for the things that he instilled in us. What made the job perfect was the fact that we could come in when we wanted to and leave at will. Sometimes Rube, Eugene, and I would work 12-hour shifts during the summer to make extra money.

It was always fun watching the boss get mad. I remember this one incident when my homeboy, Chuck, was washing Michael's new 1998 Lexus truck with the green scouring pad side of the sponge leaving scratches all over the new truck. Michael was furious and I tried not to laugh out loud, but I busted out laughing in his face…couldn't help it.

Even before Sunglow, I worked with my older brother J.C. and other close Haitian friends driving around in a white van selling boxed candy door-to-door. It was merely chump change and it didn't take a rocket scientist to know that it wasn't worth the risks we took. One day while selling candy, Fat Fritz, my best friend, was attacked by a super-sized German Sheppard. The vicious dog jumped the fence and bit him on the shoulder while he was on his knees presenting his merchandise on these folk's doorsteps in a white neighborhood. A chunk of meat was ripped off from his shoulder. These chumps had the audacity to have a teeny tiny fence for this big ol' dog. If you ask me, they should've been thrown in jail for their negligence because that dog could easily have attacked anyone walking by that house. We laughed at Fritz when he was telling us how he kept asking the owners, "Are you sure he won't jump the fence because he looks like he wants to eat me?" Fritz got a chance to turn the laughter back at me when I was attacked by five dogs a couple of weeks later. Fortunately, for me it was a cold day (60° degrees is considered cold in Florida) so I was wearing a jacket with long pants. I knocked on the door and a little white girl opened the door and left it wide open. I could see that she was watching *Beauty and the Beast*.

The girl yelled out, "Mommy, Mommy there's a boy selling candy ... can I have some?"

All I know is that out of nowhere, a pack of dogs came running towards me. I dropped my box and ran across their yard full speed. One of the dogs tripped me by running between my legs. Once on the ground, one dog got my right sleeve, one grabbed my left sleeve, another grabbed my right pant leg, yet another grabbed my left pant leg and the fifth one ran circles around me. It was as if he was cheering the other dogs on as the pack leader. I tried to shake them off while on

The Courage To Believe

the ground, but couldn't until some little boys in the area came to my rescue with their Super Soaker Water Guns spraying the dogs. The girl's mom was in the kitchen baking cookies, then finally realizing what was happening and by her saying a couple of words, they all ran back inside in obedience to their owner. She cleaned me up in her bathroom with a dog bite kit [it was on-hand as if this has happened before] and brought my whole box of candy. If she wasn't as fine as she was, I probably would've forced the issue to see how much money I could've gotten out of the situation, but she was extremely nice and kind.

Understandably, I was scared of dogs for a little while, but I eventually got over my fears pretty quickly. I love the craziness of dogs and people. Both display the basic instinct of wild animals. This was one fear of many that as a young man I was determined to be victorious over! The significance of the candy job was that we got to see outside of the hood—outside of what we thought was common. We were brought to some of the most beautiful houses and neighborhoods South Florida had to offer; neighborhoods where people took care of their yards and streets. No corner store at the end of the street, no police kicking in the doors or sirens going off every other minute, no drug dealers parading the streets, and no crack heads with cloned behaviors panhandling odd amounts like $2.56. Even though we rarely stepped a foot inside any of the homes, it always motivated me to want to acquire some of these nice things that we were able to see from the outside. One could only imagine what the inside looked like. I remember thinking to myself that this must be what going to college and getting a real good education can get people … a beautiful wife, the 2.5 kids and a lovely home, and that equaled success. I assumed this because of all the alma mater flags I had seen in those suburbs. Seeing black couples in the "nice neighborhoods" also gave me a sense of pride and I smiled gracefully on the inside whenever I was greeted by them.

The truth of the matter is that I never really knew where we were because it was my first time away from the ghetto aside from the school trips. We saw houses made with glass, fancy yards, and enough Benzes and Beamers to last a lifetime. I believe that our whole purpose of working that job was to see that there was another way to live other than the housing projects. The drama that came with it (not to say that the rich don't have drama themselves) was collateral damage that happened to come with the broadening of our horizons. In fact, the more money you have, the bigger the drama if there is no wisdom on how to make financially smart decisions.

All of us had big dreams and big goals, but the reality at the time, as it is today with the youth, was that you had to get money in the most immediate and fastest way. Most of our friends went on to sell weed while some went on to sell crack. Whatever the kids did in the neighborhood, we all made money and stood on common ground — survival.

SEVEN

FIELD OF DREAMS

My siblings and I played some kind of sport, but *my* passion was in football and track & field. I was always one of the fastest from elementary to high school. You couldn't mention the fastest runner in school without putting my name in the sentence. As early as the fourth grade at Park Ridge Elementary, all the popular boys and girls either raced each other or did back flips for competition or better yet, for bragging rights. The U.S. Olympic Gymnastics Team had nothing on them; the way they flipped and twisted in the air was outstanding. Quite impressive! I'm amazed no one broke their necks or even twisted an ankle. Mr. Everett, our P.E (Physical Education) instructor, formed a relay team consisting of who he felt were the top four fastest boys and girls in the school. Mr. Everett was a short pants wearing, shoulder length Jheri-curl having, tube socks, pencil in his ear at all times, smile on his face nearly most of the time, kind of P.E. teacher.

However, Mr. Everett over-looked me; of course in my mind, I should've *obviously* been one of the chosen ones.

So one day I stepped to Mr. Everett in his nut-hugger short pants and told him, "I could beat Keith."

Keith was a heavy-set older kid who was surprisingly fast on his feet.

"You really think you can beat him, Kevin?" He asked while laughing as is if I were joking.

That inconsiderate laughter is the reason why till this day I do not like to be laughed at. What king would? It took a lot of courage to speak up for myself. I knew he was the type of guy that would respect that from a young kid who was black like him. Being from the old school, he was the type of administrator that would let the students fight [not that he encouraged it] and the loser would get sent to the office to get internal suspension … yep, the loser. The next morning I faced my challenger Keith. We raced in a 50 yard dash (half a football field). Everybody gathered around to watch as if we were Michael Johnson and Maurice Green racing for a million bucks, but unfortunately he cheated by bumping into me when he was losing and it was a tie.

During my tenure at Crystal Lake Middle School, I waited until eighth grade before joining the track team for one season. I never had a reason why I joined other than the fact that all the popular kids in middle school were doing it, so I did too. My first race was running the 400 meters. I was so nervous that my legs were shaking at the starting line. At the end, I finished third or fourth place, but after that race, I worked hard to get better at my craft and improved tremendously. Once I crossed over into high school, the same guys that beat me in middle school couldn't touch me.

Running gave me a natural high that happened to be good for my health and confidence. If it weren't for track & field, I wouldn't have seen a way possible to go to college. I saw track

The Courage To Believe

& field as a way out of the hood along with the day-to-day hand to mouth struggles that went with life in the ghetto. That is why education is paramount to people of color because it opens so many doors that were closed to us for decades.

Now in high school, life became more harsh than usual. Fritz and I, now freshmen, practiced with the varsity football team during the summer before school started in 1995. One afternoon during the end of summer, a teacher was sexually violated in her classroom while preparing for the first day of school.

On that particular day, Fritz and I arrived late to football practice mainly because we had to get past all of the news trucks and reporters. The detectives asked our coach to identify anyone that arrived late to practice on that particular day; however, even though we were late, we were never questioned by the detectives because neither of us matched the description.

After practice, our coach explained to the whole team what this woman was going to have to go through; as far as being tested and then waiting to see if she caught HIV/AIDS or any sexually transmitted diseases and the nightmares that she would have to live with. The guy who sexually assaulted her stole her cell phone; that's how the law tracked him down a week later after he sold it. The school security system changed drastically after that horrific incident. We went from 0 to over 20 video cameras that were installed all around campus. Unfortunately, that was not the last time that we had to deal with this subject.

On the flip side, high school was a great experience. Skipping classes in high school was what you would call a social norm. Even though I took school seriously, it was hard not to skip class with my friends, especially for the skip parties. The girls would usually host these parties because guys could never be organized enough to do so, peacefully anyway. The girls would be in the kitchen gossiping and cooking chicken, rice, hot dogs, etc…you know Kool-Aid had to be close by. There was a lot of weed smoking out in the back yard and teenage drinking going on. There were guys in the living room watching a movie and cracking jokes while music played in the background and others playing cards at the table, rolling dice in the living room, and playing dominoes. People came and went all day long. It was a good venue for getting phone numbers and breaking the ice with the subject of your crush.

There would normally be an after-party after the party at my home girl Tammie's house. Unfortunately, if you were a guy and weren't invited by a female or given the privilege to stay, you would be kicked out. Even though there was a mixture of African Americans, Caucasians, and Latinos at these parties, the kind of ethnic tension that existed at other local area high schools was still lying dormant, but you could feel that something was brewing under the surface. The young ladies that were there were drunk and wanted to strip for us. They also wanted to have sex with each boy there, four of us to be exact. People were having sex in the bathroom, the kitchen floor, and the living room. Peer pressure! I didn't want to look lame in front of my friends, so I just sort of watched and laughed at them.

The Courage To Believe

The neighborhood nymphomaniac, Brenda, was there charging one dollar to have sex. Yes, one sad and lonely dollar. A dollar use to go a long way back then for some folks. You can't even get a ¼ gallon of milk for a dollar in the new millennium. Some dudes refused to pay her because they said that they would rather buy a soda and a bag of chips for that mighty dollar. Brenda was a troubled teen to be involved in such activities at a young age. She later switched schools because a picture of her sticking a Heineken bottle, bottom side up (BSU), in her vagina was being passed around. We were all 15 or 16 at the time, and these types of extracurricular activities were common around the hoods. What guy in the middle of puberty would want to miss out on that? The females were just as bad as the guys. My perception of females changed after seeing a lot of them fighting each other with razor blades hidden in their mouths during these skip parties or after school.

There were so many good memories about my freshmen year in high school. The two that stick out the most were during The *International Talent Show*, which was a pretty big deal to everyone at the school. First, at the auditions, my friend Lilda Martine sang a song from the Fugee's album, *Killing Me Softly*. I knew she could sing, but watching her on that stage singing the way she did was magnificent and sent chills down my spine. *Everybody* that was there jumped out of their seats clapping and whistling. If there were a talent scout in the audience, she would've received a record deal on the spot. By the time the talent show came along, Lilda added hip-hop to the song with my other friend, Fabine. This was a pretty cool mixture. The Brazilian girls did their act in their yellow and green native soccer jerseys with blue skintight leggings, which were very sexy. The Jamaicans did their thing, the Asians represented, but the Haitians—my group—put the icing on the cake.

"The Score" (a multi-platinum selling album) became the anthem for Haitians across the country as did the "The Fugees," a Haitian hip-hop group whom we portrayed during our school's International Talent Show. I was particularly proud of my Haitian heritage and to be able to represent The Fugees or Haitian *anything* for that matter. The Fugees made such an impact in the music industry and the exposure, which was given to my beloved Haiti, was on a positive level. The Fugees gave more creditability to Haitians across the world for the first time in a long time. Whether it was in the newspaper or on television, Haiti and Haitians were always portrayed as a filthy country or in a negative light. The local, national, and world news never bothered to share some of the more beautiful parts of our country.

Haiti is filled with breathtaking mountains, beautiful horses, nice neighborhoods with mansions, and houses on hills where there are breathtaking views of the country and eager minds running free.

I remember once in my Latin class, a classmate named Jacon't was showing us pictures of her family and their home in Haiti. Jacon't was an interesting female because she acted like her crap didn't stink and didn't care what people thought about her. She was given a brand new Mustang convertible for her 16th birthday, so it was obvious that her parents had money.

The Courage To Believe

The pictures of her parents in their mini mansion opened a lot of people's eyes, including mine, that life in Haiti wasn't one of poverty for everyone, which was how the media normally portrayed it.

One Hispanic peer made a comment with a big smile on his face, "Haiti don't have houses like that!" That comment got under my skin a little more than I'd like to admit. Even though I had never been to Haiti, the fire that burned in my heart for my parents' homeland was deep. As I perched my mouth to trample on his snide comment, Jacon't beat me to the count. She gave him a piece of her mind in a graceful, but in an acerbic manner. It just so happened that this kid used to get jumped by Haitian boys in middle school so I'm assuming the animosity was still there.

In my group, there were five dance couples. The girls had on their homemade Caribbean outfits, which consisted of red skirts with black tights underneath and a matching headpiece wrapped around their heads. The boys had on red, collared shirts with khaki pants. The dance routine that we performed was different from what we auditioned with which was the clean version. We knew upfront that the administrators didn't want any bumping and grinding, but we bumped, grinded, and gyrated anyway during our actual performance.

The whole process from beginning to end was a lot of fun. Most of our group was juniors and seniors except for the fresh meat: Me, Charlene and Shasha Harris, who was Jamaican…the only non-Haitian in the group. Shasha was arguably the finest freshman on campus. She always wore expensive name brand clothes and dated the sports stars of the school. I never approached her because I felt that she was out of my league. After our performance I didn't have to approach her because she came to me and wanted to be friends. Unfortunately, I never got the chance to strike up a relationship because she transferred to another high school.

The talent show made me so proud to be Haitian—the proudest point still to this day. We really felt like royalty because it seemed that the audience loved our dance performance and, as a result, we received a standing ovation. The crowd just went wild! Unfortunately, there was so much fighting between faculty and the student body as to whom had the controlling rights over reproduction and projected sales of the video recording that once the dust settled, the video tape of the talent show was supposedly destroyed and, therefore, never reproduced. The "Power of Greed" in action.

The exposure made me popular and my dates picked up substantially from third round ladies to first round draft picks. I must admit, my ego was definitely inflated. Suddenly, good-looking, upper-class females wanted to chill with me. If only I was actively chasing girls at the time, but I was oblivious to matters of seduction had turned my attention to class work. I had to set the example for my siblings. The few fellas I hung around with on and off campus: Ronald, Mike, Joe, Fritz, Spade, and J-Styles were able to get more girls because of me. Our hang out spot changed from loitering outside by the buses to cracking jokes on each other in the main hallway where the older students roamed. We earned our passage there by rite of popularity.

The Courage To Believe

Sophomore year was a bang. I excelled in football, however my bread and butter were track & field. I loved going to track meets because I've always said that the finest women in the world ran track. Track requires muscle tone in all the right places. Besides the hormones, I really enjoyed the natural high of heart pumping, skin sweating, and adrenaline accelerating while running the field. Deerfield High was very cheap when it came to track. So cheap that the school's officials let go one of the best track coaches in Florida and probably the nation, Coach Snider. He went to a school out west in Coral Springs that paid him more and he wasn't hesitant about saying it. Once he left, the spirit of the track program fell into a drought; only the true warriors of the sport stayed. I had the pleasure of running with some pretty good athletes. We had a cheap running track made of concrete and painted lines, but we did what we could with it. The show had to go on!

I was skinny, about 140 pounds with a great deal of heart for the sport. Dedication and ambition were two things that I never lacked… ever. I had to have a good practice every day or it would beat me mentally. There was a particular practice that my coach was hard on me about because of a conditioning workout that the team was doing. I kept messing up for some reason. We were supposed to run around the track for a mile by sprinting 100 yards, jog around the curve for another 100 yards, sprint 100 yards, and then jog another 100 yards four times equaling one mile. I was dog-tired after that practice, but I came back that night to the track field to do it all over again until I was satisfied. I was crazy like that because I was determined to prevail. It was dark and creepy out there that night without even a dim beam of light, but the mission was completed.

Sports were basically a mental thing just like life because anything in life that is worth having is worth the extra effort to go after until it is yours. Whether it's college, a companion, a family, a house, or a yacht! The ability to focus helped me put my issues in perspective. No matter what the circumstance, moving forward is what I'll always advise anyone ... regardless of your status is in society, rich or poor - always focus on your dreams. As determined as I was, the devil wasn't too far behind; he showed himself in the artificial strife Americans had against Haitians.

Summertime was coming around and the Haitian vs. American beef was cooking up all over again. These battles made my high school football career a nightmare because most of the team were Black Americans that had an ignorant, biased mentality against Haitians and the other half were Haitians, a few Hispanics, and Caucasians. Back and forth the team would be fighting each other, in the locker room, on the field, off the field and in the middle of practice as well. As I saw it, there was never a unified team, just a group of young men wearing the same uniform trying to get scholarships. I just couldn't commit myself to an organization that was discriminating against each other *within* each other. Both sides were wrong. No matter how hard I tried to stay neutral, I couldn't.

At the beginning of summer school, Fritz, Eugene and I were expelled from school for defending ourselves. There had to be at least ten Americans trying to jump us in front of the school and three of them were on the football team. The cameras saw everything. All the administrators had to do was look at the video recording to know that we were defending ourselves. They were fed up with the fights that were breaking out in the classrooms and during lunch. The previous year in1995, the Broward County School Board created a policy that gave the school's administration permission to expel at their discretion any student that was 16 or over, whether it was for poor grades, fighting, excessive tardiness, or absences. The school went through a summer makeover by kicking out anyone who they thought were a "Menace to Education."

Most of the menaces were student athletes (football or basketball players) that got back in after pleading their case to the coaches. It must be understood that there's a lot of money involved in high school sports, especially football and basketball. High career positions in the school board systems can be made or taken away depending on the success of a school's athletics, especially in sports like football or basketball that draw in large crowds. If we (Fritz, Eugene, and I) weren't on the football team, not to mention track & field, we would've had to transfer to another school A.S.A.P! In that case I would've gone to Ely High, even though Ely and Deerfield were archrivals, since most of my childhood friends went to that school. No matter what the sporting event was, as long as it was Deerfield vs. Ely, it was guaranteed to be a sold out event—a "ghetto fabulous" event to be exact. We would get new outfits, haircuts and hairdo's, and detail our cars until the finish shined like glass just for these rivalry games. Get there early or good luck with parking!

In my eyes, athletics was my ticket out of the ghetto. So I forced myself to go to class 90 percent of the time. Some of my friends were skipping classes way too much and they motivated me to do the opposite, especially since I grew out of following the pack. The other 10 percent of my time was spent whispering in girls' ears in an attempt to get them aroused.

A few of my fellow friends started selling crack, carjacking, burglarizing, and doing robberies. I saw what crack did to our people and what it was doing to our community so naturally I didn't want any part of it. Families became unstable and the rotating doors of the criminal system kept sucking up my peers. I guess you can say that I had a guilty conscience about it at the time. As a juvenile, I did a couple of break-ins and thefts stealing items such as bikes and remote control cars like the "Hammer."

Chuck, one of my boys, and one of the few Yanks that I hung out with was cool and intriguing. He was an amazing running back and also a good friend. Watching him play was entertaining; I've never seen O.J. Simpson play football other than on highlight clips, but I bet it was something similar to the feeling that Chuck gave his spectators. We watched him dance around or plow through defenders full speed into the end zone. He lived in the projects next to mine; a true hustler because he had a job working with us at Sun Glow while also selling dope. Seeing how much money he would stack up almost convinced me to start slinging, but I remained focused on my straight path to the finish line.

The Courage To Believe

We would go shopping and on double dates and he would always insist that it was all on him. He was very generous and loyal to his friends. This young man had two cars and wasn't even 16 yet. Chuck would get arrested and released within three hours because of the fact that he was a star on the varsity football team as a freshman. I remember how I used to drive with him to catch his licks (crack fiend customers). On one of our many adventurous lick trips, there was an older white lady about 65-years-old who cashed an $800 welfare check only to give it all to Chuck. Every penny of it!

At that moment, I witnessed firsthand the power of crack and the power of money. Crack was strong enough to make an old woman give up all her funds for the month, to purchase a drug that would only give her a temporary high. The money made Chuck happy to the point that he would degrade himself by taking advantage of an old woman that was helpless. When crack and money converge, people have no regard for themselves or their families. The people who supplied the drugs had no limit to what they would do for the cash so there was a symbiotic relationship between seller and user.

The police would sometimes arrest Chuck on possession of rocks and then call the head coach to come to the police station to get him (barely anyone knew about this). I would always tell him to leave the drug game saying, "You are going to be worth millions five years from now." He would do what he always did which was laugh out loud. Eventually, Chuck got caught in another city, Ft. Lauderdale, which landed him a first class ticket to prison. All the V.I.P. treatment stopped once he quit playing ball.

Another classmate of mine for many years had an older brother who, along with a couple of his friends, was sentenced to 25 years for manslaughter of a drug fiend that owed them money. They stomped the guy to death. They were only 13 years old at the time and will probably be released by 2020. Stories like these come a dime a dozen where I am from.

In low-income neighborhoods you never know what's going to happen next. I remember the infamous summer night of June 28, 1997, when Mike Tyson fought Holyfield and bit off his ear. As excited as that seemed, my neighborhood had its own drama unraveling. A schoolmate of mine named Eddie, R.I.P., was shot and killed the same night of the fight. I was 17 years old and was watching the fight a couple of blocks away from home. Either we didn't have cable or the cable man would always catch us stealing it. At the same time I was being dropped off after watching the fight, a swarm of police and emergency response crewmembers came charging into my complex.

The sound of the sirens brightened the dark streets. Knowing that my mom and siblings were at home, I was praying they weren't headed to my place. My breathing suddenly stopped! Slowly I exhaled a sigh of relief when the swarm of police and emergency vehicles halted at the front of the complex and not at the back where I lived. Thank God it didn't.

Eddie was a star wrestler and also the friend of a young lady who had a "butch or femme" as a girlfriend. He was the kind of guy you could always count on for a good laugh. Eddie and the young lady were sitting in the front of the apartment under the dim street light smoking weed. He was standing there, chilling with his friend when her femme came by.

"You better not be here when I get back," the butch told him with a threatening tone.

"Yeah, whatever!"

Eddie never moved an inch.

Fifteen minutes later, "What the hell…?" said Eddie, startled to see the butch with the gun's chrome gleaming in the night.

Eddie ran to the apartment behind him. He tried to open the windows, but he didn't know how to open the security bars in the apartment (you would have to squeeze the two knobs together and pull the screen up- something that nobody would figure out on the first try or in a panic). He finally tried to hide in the closet, but his pursuer closed in on him.

Boom! She killed him with one shot at point blank range and then went outside where her girlfriend was and yelled out, "I love you," bang…killing herself as well. The news headlines read, "Murder-Suicide."

We were already in the process of moving into our first home, but we rushed it by a couple of weeks not because of the recent deaths, but because I also got into a fight defending a "Just Come," also known as a J.C., which is a person who just arrived from Haiti. I defended the freshman from Douglas, an

American so-called bully. He wasn't targeting his jokes on the freshman Just Come alone, but at my culture as a whole, at every Haitian who was in the swimming class. I wasn't having that—period. Examples of ignorant comments would be "Haitians can't dress, why they always coming over here stinking up our school or of course, the most famous one…H.B.O. (Haitian Body Odor)," etc.

Eddie's death was still fresh in my system so I still had residual hostility left in me from an old friend dying so violently. I guess that's why folks in the ghetto can be mean because we often lose loved ones so violently to the streets and to vicious crimes that pollute the community. Those feelings make you want to get revenge, but revenge on whom or what exactly…on the systems that perpetuate the poverty that breeds such senseless violence? That's an enemy that can't be caught in a net or captured under a jar. Perhaps the root of frustration in the ghetto lies in the fact that the desire for revenge on this invisible enemy is never truly satisfied. Instead, a few shift the blame onto flesh and blood enemies whom we can see, littering the streets with the bodies of their own neighbors; an act that only further entrenches us in a maze of crime, homicide, prison traps, etc. I think we all have that urge for revenge, but thankfully few of us act upon such a dangerous feeling.

I asked Douglas nicely to chill out picking on the man, but he wanted to impress the girls, so then he started messing with me. He was messing with the wrong person at the wrong time. It was the last week of school and I had enough self-control to wait patiently until the last day. Since he wasn't in my face trash talking, I decided to teach him a lesson after final exams. Patience is a virtue. Douglas was going to be in for a first degree, old school butt whooping because it was surely premeditated by me, of course. I worked out by lifting weights and shadow boxing in order to get that extra strength over Douglas who had a weight advantage over me. We played on the football team together so I knew he was pretty strong, but I wasn't any weakling.

When the last day of school came, I hunted for Douglas until I spotted him heading toward the front gates of the school. I waited for him to get two steps from me and then said, "You going to *respect* Haitians!" He only had time to say, "What?" before I unloaded an army of punches. I really let him have it. His mouth was leaking blood covering his gold teeth. Next thing I knew, a cop grabbed us by our shirts real tight, almost choking me as he pulled us away. I shook loose and ran through my projects across the street with a motorcycle cop chasing me. I jumped this eight-foot wall hundreds of times, but that day I was dog tired from fighting and running, barely rolling over the wall after a second attempt. A roofer, who was working on one of the apartments, saw me and told the cops where I was hiding. The cop was pretty good at maneuvering the bike through the grass. I jumped up and rolled back over the wall with the little energy I had left, but he got me.

The cop said, "Kiddo, you're pretty fast."

I replied, "Yeah, thanks…I just finished track season."

EIGHT

THE PALM BEACHES

The move to Boynton Beach, FL. in Palm Beach County was exciting because it was our first actual house. There were three bedrooms, two bathrooms, central air with a huge corner-lot yard boasting two large palm trees in the front and flowers everywhere; it was beautiful. The first thing we noticed as young adult males were the large number of young adult females that resided in the area and good looking too. Unfortunately, we were warned that there was a high rate of STD's (Sexually Transmitted Diseases) at Santaluces High, which was the local high school. This was a fact: Most schools in South Florida were battling the STD epidemic.

As exciting as the move to Boynton Beach was, it was extremely boring compared to our last neighborhood and the myriad of street entertainment. I immediately understood why there was so much sexual activity in the area and adjacent communities; what else would teens that were bored to tears do for fun? Once we adjusted to our new surroundings and made new friends, invitations to parties and local hang out spots began pouring in and we began to have a little fun.

Santaluces High School had a beautiful rubber track field that was black with bright red stripes. I noticed it right away when I joined their football squad. My mind was already on track & field, but football season had just started. Focusing on what's ahead was nothing new to me; that's usually the norm.

The Courage To Believe

The difference between their athletic program and my old high school's athletic program was very noticeable. This school had money…lots of it, and wasn't cheap with anything regarding their student athletes. The locker room itself was the size of a college team locker room. The students there loved Master P, a rapper from Louisiana, and the whole "No Limit" movement. One could hardly go an entire class period without somebody uttering Master P's trademark moan, "Uhhh…N-nah-n-nah!" Every male, whether they were black, white, or Hispanic thought they were Mama Mia, Silk the Shocker, or C-Murder (members of "No Limit," the rap group from Louisiana). There were too many pretty boys to count, but I had to admit these dudes knew how to dress. Before I even knew of my mother's plans to move to Boynton, I heard about the area and that it was a good place to rob folks because of the abundance of cash on hand. Robbing wasn't my thing, but I hung around a few "jack boys." The hood had many talents, but fortunately, I wasn't interested in finding out if mine was behind a ski mask with a gun in my hands. My passion was in sports—I loved football, but track & field was my dream.

The coaches loved my tenacity, but wished that I had practiced with them over the summer "two-a-days" (practicing twice a day for five days) to learn their defensive playbook. Missing out on those intensive practice sessions made it impossible for me to have a starting position – it would not have been fair. I used football as a tool to let off my frustration of being away from Pompano, my hometown. At first, I really hated being in Boynton Beach, but I got used to it once the Haitian community opened their arms to us. "Deerfield" was my nickname and jersey number 25 was given to me. I was very good at playing safety and was accepted by most of the players expect for Darvious, a senior who had a serious problem with me. As it was, before I became a part of the team, I had already intruded upon his starting position as safety and he was feeling the heat from the possibility of losing his position to a transfer student. We actually fought a couple of times during practice because he allowed his friends on the team to get into his head. He didn't *completely* lose his position to me, but I was allowed to start 3 out of 10 games. One night after practice, a coach from the team came by my house to tell me that there was a lot of politics between the coaches on whether I should have the starting position. They concluded that even though I practiced twice as hard, their main concern at that point was Darvious. Since he was a senior, they needed to give him the extra boost in getting into a good football program with a full scholarship. As disappointing as the sound was to my ear, I had to respect the coaches' decision and their genuine concern for our college future that wasn't present at my home school. Darvious and I eventually became cool after the season, as we were both on the 4 x 4 relay track team. Of course, without a doubt, I was the superior athlete.

Eager to go out and mingle, I teamed up with Pro, Charlie, and Nine who were all Haitian and also related to one other. Pro was the player out of the group. He had girls for days and his mom would allow him to have sex in the house while she was there. Most guys with Haitian parents would sneak their girls in, but not Pro. His mom, Claire, was cool with everything he did. She was very *down* ... a little too *down*. Charlie and Nine were brothers and while Charlie was deemed the good one, Nine would be out running the streets.

The Courage To Believe

They had a real nice mom named Zamene, who was also an excellent cook of Caribbean cuisine.

I got oral sex for the first time while chilling with Charlie, Pro, and Nine at this young lady's house. The young lady that was providing the service was mad at me and quit because I kept pulling her head down. Since she was Pro's girlfriend, he talked her into finishing the job. We had a lot of fun hanging out together … parties, clubs, and even church together, but eventually, like they say, "All good things must come to an end."

Under the track coaching staff at Santaluces High, I developed, or should I say, perfected my running form. My time dropped substantially in the 400 meters from 51 and 52 seconds to 49 and 48 (48.8 – personal best) seconds. Track & Field is a team sport, but it's a sport that also gives an individual time to shine. Boy, did I shine my tail off! I became real strong and bulky and had an eight pack. The girls couldn't wait to catch me with my shirt off, literally. Back then I was doing five hundred sit-ups a day and about three to four hundred pushups five times a week. College scouts were attending our track practices and noticed my tenacious work ethic and were asking me questions. I remember practicing as hard as a horse, showing off whenever there was a scout present because Coach George would give us a heads up (something that I never experienced at my old high school and I really appreciated).

Athletically, Santaluces was the perfect school because their athletic program stressed the future of their student athletes. Even though I was missing Deerfield High, they only cared about what we were able to do on the field for them, compared to Santaluces who forced juniors to take the initiative to call up different colleges. They even provided the athletes with professional, full body massages free of charge. They treated me like royalty, just like the other star athletes. Every school shows some kind of favoritism toward one or two athletes, but the Chiefs had an abundance of talent and raw speed amongst the athletes (must have been something in the water). In the only year that I attended Santaluces High, three of those students eventually went on to the NFL: Vincent Wilfork/New England Patriots, Clinton Jones (C.J.)/New England Patriots, and Korey Banks/Miami Dolphins.

As evidence to their pool of talent, nearly the whole track team went to the high school state finals (90 percent of the team). One would think because their district was predominately white that the competition wasn't strenuous, but the team stood tall against the predominately black Broward and Dade County schools. That is a huge statement being that we are talking about South Florida, "Home of the Speed Breeds." The Girls 4x1, 4x4, and a couple other female athletes went as individuals in almost every event: the 100, 200, 400, and 800 mile, shot put, long jump, high jump, triple jump, and hurdles. It was remarkable!

On the boys side there was the same caliber of talent. I was the starter in the 4x4 along with Arrington/2nd leg, Brown/3rd leg, and C.J., who was the fastest, ran anchor leg. Even though I ran the first leg of the 4x4, I didn't make it as an individual in the 400 meters that year. In the 4x4, we came in

The Courage To Believe

third (out of eight schools), which was good enough for a medal. I was blessed just to be in that environment. Our anchor, C.J., was one of the most talented individuals I've ever met. He won second place in both the 400 meters and 200 meters as a junior. There's no need to elaborate on what he did as a senior.

Prior to the 1998 track and field state finals, I revealed to my teammates that I would be returning to my old stomping ground, Deerfield High. This prompted C.J. and some of my other teammates to make a friendly bet with me that I wouldn't make it to state finals the following school year without them. Everybody wanted me to stay, but most understood that I had to graduate where my heart was. Now looking back, I can admit that it was a bad move for my athletic career. With their coaching tactics, college scouts, and NFL contacts, my chances of turning pro as a track or football athlete would have been much higher at Santaluces. The 2008 Olympic Games of Beijing would've even been a possibility. I could only imagine.

> *I've learned that in life, whenever you are in a set place and God's grace surrounds you and His blessings abounds towards* you; *you will experience sweat-less victory.*

I should've listened to my mom. I've learned that in life, whenever you are in a set place and God's grace surrounds you and His blessings abounds towards you, YOU will experience sweat-less victory and excel, therefore, you should remain there until God moves you. We often, as I have done time after time, forfeit our inheritance of prosperity, leaving our gifts, while we head towards traps placing us in the wrong place at the wrong time.

Following after my heart's love and sentiment, I eventually would go back to Deerfield for my senior year. I grew up across the street and felt that I just had to finish there with the people I grew up and went to school with. I literally begged my mom to let me go back because she initially was set against it. Our parents are charged with the responsibility of knowing what's best and are usually right. I would consistently ask her to let me transfer back so we made a deal. She said if I finished the year with nothing lower than a B, she would get me a car so that I could drive back and forth to school that was about 15 miles (a 20 to 25 minute drive every day). If I didn't get the good grades, I would have to stay and graduate at Santaluces High. We both kept our end of the bargain and off I went to the "Home of the Bucks."

I made a couple friends during my short tenure at Santaluces High, but didn't realize the impact I had on some of them until they knew my plan of departure was for real. One person in particular that I knew would be missed was a princess named Sarah—Sarah Fredricks. She was a track mate and classmate of mine. Sarah was like a teenager stuck in a full-fledged woman's mind and body; a one in a million type of person. She was beautiful, extremely intelligent, and had a backside that would break a guy's neck for looking too hard. The icing on the cake was that she was a Haitian Princess and wore a necklace around her neck that said so. We had one class together-Marine Biology and I noticed her from the first day I stepped into the crowded classroom.

The Courage To Believe

We had only one real conversation. That one conversation took place after a track practice and it sparked a match filled with the fire of passion. Sarah was the type of female that dudes dreamed of being with. The other guys were a pack of hyenas, I was the lone lion, and she was the prey, so to speak. Of course, the lion heart always wins. She had no idea how much of a crush I had on her, but what threw me off was that her best friend, Stephanie, revealed to a mutual friend that Sarah also had a crush on me. What a coincidence! I smiled from ear to ear.

One day leaving the locker room after a spring football game, I walked by a group of girls (Sarah and Stephanie were in the group), and one of the girls started singing "U Make Me Wanna," a hit song by Usher with a big smile on her face. The song was about Usher wanting to leave the girl he was with for her gal pal that he befriended for advice about their current relationship.

When I walked past the girls, the song remained in my head and then I realized that they were singing the song because I had a girlfriend and someone told Sarah that I wanted to be with her instead. That was true all the way around because Sarah gave me advice on how to deal with my relationship issues during our lunch break. My secret feelings for Sarah were almost enough to keep me at Santaluces. At the end of our final exams, we exchanged numbers, vowed to keep in touch, took a picture together and went on our separate ways.

Months later, going back to Deerfield High was like a homecoming. A lot of love was shown to me. It was as if I returned from exile to claim my throne; not to mention the noticeable jealousy from a few of the "in" crowd. I had a red beeper back then that I called my hotline because of the way people would blow it up with different codes. One female that I began to get involved with was Queta who would beep me the most and gave me a sheet of paper containing the meaning of all the codes. It was kind of cute.

She was a cheerleader and had a 'cuteness' about her that I overlooked with my newly inflated ego since my return. I remember how rude I use to be towards her by hanging up on her in the middle of conversations, ignoring her, and talking to other females in front of her. She was determined to have me as her man and she won. We shared a lot with each other and she turned out to be my first love. Whatever she needed, I gave to her and vice versa. She had me wrapped around her finger.

During that year, Queta brought to my attention that her friend Melissa, also a cheerleader, was sexually assaulted by a teammate on the football team. Darnell was his name, and I heard a few similar rumors about him, "taking pussy" (raping), but never paid too much attention because I didn't hang around him or his crowd. The boys would always joke about the rumors, but I never found them funny. The fact that we both played on defense and he led our team prayers most of the time infuriated me. (I would keep my eyes open when he prayed.) This situation alone made me regret leaving Santaluces at times.

Melissa was a very attractive female that was from Brazil. Most of her life was a disaster because her father molested her throughout her childhood. As a result, it left her emotionally imbalanced and constantly depressed. My girl Queta and Melissa became good friends over the years once they met at a private Catholic school, moving together to a public school and ultimately joining the high school cheerleading team simultaneously. One day, she stopped by his house and he quickly took advantage of her as Queta waited outside in her car in front of his house. Maybe as a predator Darnell, was able to smell Melissa's vulnerability emanating from her lack of self-esteem.

Witnessing the effect of what happened to Melissa started to bother me because Queta was affected. It was a domino effect. Even though Darnell hadn't done anything directly to me, I wanted to punish him. A couple of my fellas and I went to his house and used a girl to knock on his door. We knew that he would open the door because he was a pervert and pried on innocent girls. The perfect war strategy is to use your foe's weakness to trap them.

We rushed in, beat him with bats, and set the house on fire by throwing gasoline-filled beer bottles through the windows and around the house. I'll admit that the fire part was a bit extreme, but I don't think it was my idea. I just felt like he was pure evil. He misused quotes from the bible to downgrade women, but here I am trying to burn someone's house down. I was definitely an action junky back in my teenage days because I can remember the adrenaline rush of the whole incident and how good it made me feel—street justice. We were all lucky that none of us were caught, but that would've been an honorable case to catch.

Melissa ended up dropping the charges against Darnell due to threats he made to her while she was at work. I can't explain how angry this made those of us who knew about the situation, but I had to respect it and keep it moving in order to focus on the rest of the school year—senior year. As much as it was rumored that he was a rapist, I thought that it was only a matter of time before the law was going to get him, if AIDs didn't. He's someone that I know will be on Court TV or A&E in the future, if he isn't doing a prison bid now for multiple sexual assaults. I wish I had dealt with him accordingly when I had the chance, especially since my friends wanted to kill him that night. I sometimes feel partly responsible for the females that were violated by him after Melissa.

This creep switched into my Literature class during the last semester of school; it was my favorite class, one of them anyway, and I didn't want that bastard in my presence. I spoke with Dr. Mailto, the principal of the school, who was well aware of the allegations and knew me by name because of my popularity in athletics. He told me that he couldn't promise anything, but two days after we met, Darnell was switched to another class. That's power! I'm thankful to Dr. Mailto that I didn't have to be the one to leave that class as I never would've learned about Macbeth (my favorite Shakespeare play).

Even though I hate to admit it, the events around my girlfriend and her best friend broke us up. My football career suffered enough. I had no confidence on the field because I was there physically, but wasn't there mentally. It was too stressful and neither of us could focus so we separated, but I didn't feel complete without her since I was truly in love with her.

Track season came along with some fresh air. Our track team was small, but I enjoyed it because most of us were seniors. Wilson Sherman was our head coach. He was a tall, black man with an intimidating look about him. He had a very strict coaching style and at times seemed unfair, but he got the job done. I was surprised that he was an elementary school teacher. Coach Sherman had this quote that he would always say to us, "No matter what you go through remember that someone somewhere got through it and you will too!" This quote is something that he brainwashed into our heads, but in a good way because every time I fell, I knew that getting back up separated me from the weak.

The women's side of the squad consisted of Sabine, Trail, Guilda, Lotus, Black, and Easter. The men's side consisted of Greg, Robert, O.Z., Todd, Vincent, and Head (forgive me if I forgot anyone). Coach Corey was the assistant coach, but had been helping us for years at the school and should've been the head coach. Instead, the school went out of their way to hire a new head coach. Sabine, Trail, Black, and I went to the state finals and the results were nothing to brag about. I did horribly, but the fact that I made it was enough for me due to the circumstances.

I never won the "big race," in the 400 meters, at the district, regional, or state finals. The one time I had the chance to win and was pretty close was at the 1999 regional track at Boyd Anderson (B.A.) High School in Fort Lauderdale, FL.

There were two quarter horses that I was worried about beating me in the race: Todd Devote (from B.A.) and ex-teammate C.J. Even though Todd beat me earlier that year, I wasn't too concerned with losing to him again as I was with C.J. since he had faster times than both of us. Todd had me on alert, but I wasn't scared of giving it my best shot and that's exactly what I did. I watched this guy clock a 47.5 (his fastest time) and my fastest was a 48.8 in the 400. I easily beat Todd without breaking a sweat in the preliminary race, putting me on a spiritual high for the rest of the evening. But I knew prime time would be in the finals with Todd, C.J. and I on the track and everyone wanted to see this race. The Sun-Sentinel and other local newspapers were building up the momentum of the showdown between the three of us.

My high school had a famous broadcasting program that recorded all our track meets and athletic events. A freshman was selected to record the regional track meet on her first off campus assignment. I couldn't believe that they would send such an inexperienced camera girl to an event of such magnitude. She arrived hours late and missed my two biggest races at Regionals along with everyone else's. She arrived right when my big showdown started. The race was so fast that she didn't get to focus the camera in time, but she tried ... I caught a glimpsed of my legs and red shorts. I took second place after a dude from Flanagan High School came out from the middle-of-nowhere. We exchanged leads three times. The race was a neck-to-neck finish and they had to do a photo finish to determine the winner between us. That race was so exciting! Running that fast felt as though I had wings.

The Courage To Believe

Only four of us made it to the State Finals, which was held at the University of Florida (UF). I was proud to be part of it for the second time, but the treatment that we received was appalling. Our high school only gave the coach enough money to pay for a cheap low class motel and a couple of meals (unless the coach was cuffing the cash which I seriously doubt). The motel was so dingy that one of the girls, Black, started crying upon arrival. Looking at the situation and at her made me want to shed a tear out of anger, but I was a senior and had to keep my two cents in my pocket as a leader. So we just sucked it up because we had to mentally prepare for war at the State Finals that was within 48 hours. And yet, there we were—ushered into filthy rooms with so many nasty cockroaches. Was this what the school thought of us? Was this what they believed we would be comfortable enough with?

Bugs were in the sink and bathtub, and the door locks were falling apart. One of the girls had a small video camera and recorded the conditions that we were forced to live in. If camera phones were around back then, I'm sure it would have been posted all over the social media networks. Coach Sherman had his thumb up his butt because he refused to use his money to get us into better quarters to lay our heads down, knowing that it would be refunded to him by our parents. Sabine's parents just happened to be in Gainesville for an open house at U.F. and offered to pay for our rooms somewhere else, but the coach denied the offer. Her mother and father, Pastor Deliniore, pastor of the church that I grew up in as a child, were as disgusted as we were. Sabine could have easily ditched us for the fancy hotel room with her parents at the Marriott, but being the genuinely good person she was, we all "thugged" it out together.

There were talks of a lawsuit against the school by all of our parents because we were black and this was a clear case of discrimination. Even the coaches back home felt the same way, but the incident never saw a day in court. Not to my surprise, none of us did well at the state finals. Mentally we were distracted and knocked off focus due to our temporary living situation. We didn't have an equal opportunity to be prepared for an event of such magnitude like the other student athletes and it showed. I barely received a medal at fifth place with a time that I clocked plenty of times as a junior. Despite all of the confusion, I was proud of the team and was privileged to take part of the State Finals.

NINE

SARAH SMILE

In the midst of the State Finals aftermath, the slum-like, somber experience that was supposed to be a memory for young athletes to treasure, a beautiful thing happened. Like the calm after the storm ... the moment when fierce winds give way to a calming, gentle breeze and the sun peeks through the clouds, I bumped into Sarah again at a gas station (believe it or not, back then gas was $1.00 a gallon). From inside the car, I was looking down rolling up a blunt on my lap when I saw a glimpse of a fine female. When I looked up, I saw it was her and called out her name. She ran up to me and gave me a big hug with one leg up behind her ... just like the movies! She probably would've kissed me if it weren't for her dad looking right at us. We exchanged numbers once again.

My 18th birthday was around the corner. I spent all of it with Queta, but all I could think about was Sarah. I barely called her because I wanted to step to her with a clean plate. Prom was coming up and I didn't want to go with Queta, due to our negative vibe, even though she deserved to be there with me.

The day of the prom was going perfect up until a couple of hours before it started. The stereo system in the Jaguar blew. My brother Rube and I were going crazy trying to find someone to fix the stereo system and an hour after the prom started, it was fixed. My outfit was an Italian, sea foam (green) suit with navy blue shoes that had gold lion heads. I felt like a $million$

bucks! Sarah wore a glittery red dress that gave her curves plenty of justice. We were almost two hours tardy, but made a grand, fashionably late entrance with all eyes on us. And when I showed up at the prom in a Jaguar on 20's with Sarah, everybody was knocked off balance, especially the future tabloid subscribers. No one really knew what was going on behind the curtains between Queta and I, and that's how we wanted it.

Sarah and I danced the night away because that's all we could do since we completely missed the dinner. It didn't bother me because I never leave home without eating something first. That year, the R&B singer Usher had the number one album in the world, *My Way*, and my favorite song called "Nice and Slow" began to play. We were dancing so close I was sweating like a pimp in church. Our eyes met and we kissed in the middle of the dance floor. It was a magical Disney moment and a love scene that even a picture couldn't capture. I knew someone was going to tell my ex about it, but I didn't care because I was enjoying my senior prom. Chances were that she was at home crying up a storm. The thought of that made it difficult to enjoy the night at first.

After the prom we went to a private beach. We sat on the sand trying to eat some ice cream, but the dress she had on was too skimpy to keep her warm. Her skin was so smooth and sensitive that the breezy wind made it hard for us to make out on the sand with her shivering. Eventually we went to the back seat of the Jag for privacy that led to "man on base" for the first time and I thought for sure we were going to have sex. However, being the woman that she was, the panties weren't

The Courage To Believe

going anywhere! Sarah was eighteen and only had sex once, which was three years prior. I can vouch for that.

I knew she wanted to do more than just kiss and hug me because she had this erotic look in her eyes and she made a sound with her mouth as if she was in a joyful pain, almost like a hiss of a snake, but she fought the demons that night. It must be understood that Sarah was a classy lady and I respected her mind and body for it. She was smart, sexy, knew how to cook, and wanted more out of life than just a high school diploma ... a young lady of integrity.

The year 1999 was definitely a year to remember. It was graduation morning and I woke up on time, but someone wrinkled up my shiny, red graduation gown. It was so difficult for me to smooth out the wrinkles, but my auntie Gettie came to my rescue. My little brother Pharo wanted to ride with me, so we took off down I-95 in my tough 1983 Camry. Already late for graduation and knowing the ceremony would take at least two hours, leaving us starving by the time it was over, I decided to stop by Burger King and grab a bite for the both of us. When we got to the Broward Center for the Performing Arts in downtown Fort Lauderdale, FL, the seniors were already walking into the auditorium. My last name, which begins with a D, gave me a chance to walk right into my spot in the line before the person in front of me walked into the main section—smooth operator. The following Sunday, I got *baptized* for the first time, voluntarily.

Mom threw me the biggest party on this side of the Mississippi. I didn't even want the party because of the financial burden it was going to put on her, but I'm glad she didn't listen to me. The turnout was so huge that I had to end it before the walls of our home came down. Everybody had a good time even though a couple of fights almost broke out. There was a new club scheduled to open on the same night as my party. I was approached by some of the club representatives suggesting that I switch my party to their club instead. Since we were holding events on the same night, they wanted me to have my party at their club and, of course, charge my guests an admission fee so their club could earn revenue. Although I knew rejecting their request would make us enemies, I turned down their offer anyway so that everyone would have fun for free—a real party. Those same guys came to my party and allegedly were the ones who dropped a stink bomb in my home causing everyone to *leave* the house gasping for air, but not *leave* the party. I guess they expected everyone to head to their club. Instead, their plans backfired and my party got even bigger since the people driving by saw that there was a huge party going down outdoors. The D.J. diffused the situation by playing the Juvenile 1999 hit song, "Back That Thang Up;" the crowd went crazy and ran back inside. We had so much fun and the food was terrific, thanks to my mom, Auntie Gettie and the help of some of the mothers in neighborhood – spreading love like an African village. I also got a chance to meet, for the first time, some of my cousins from Miami: Leon, Gary and Seg. We've remained very close over the years.

By sunrise, my father showed up to congratulate me. I was definitely surprised by his visit because it had been a few years since I'd seen him. My mother wanted me to give him a graduation ticket, but I refused to because he wasn't a part of

The Courage To Believe

our struggle. I must admit that there was some animosity toward him; however, I eventually forgave him years later. My father wasn't the only surprise that day.

My family was cleaning up the mess around the house when I got a call from my boss at Sam's Club. I knew I had the day off because I requested it so that my folks wouldn't be cleaning up by themselves, not to mention the anticipated hangover from the holy water and grass that my friends and family enjoyed in the backyard.

My supervisor Tom called me and asked, "Why aren't you at your cash register today?"

I replied, "It's my day off," explaining to him that I requested the day off for my graduation party and it was granted by the assistant manager.

Everybody knew that I was having a party because I promoted it even while I was at work to my co-workers and every fine female that I bumped into. Tom said that he would call me back after finding out whether I was telling the truth or not. I knew that I wasn't lying because I really enjoyed that job; it was the first time that I really felt a part of a team at a multi-billion dollar franchise. Less than five minutes later, the manager called back and said that the assistant manager said that I never requested the day off and not to come back to work.

Wow ... Just my luck to get fired on my day off! Mom told me not to forget what was done to me, but to take it as a lesson to get educated and become my own boss. Somehow, some way, her words of wisdom always made us feel better, no matter how minor or drastic the situation. I still hear her words of guidance like a whisper in the wind.

TEN

LOVE, PEACE AND GOOD FOOD

With high school and graduation behind me, I didn't know where I was going to college. I settled down and was admitted to the University of South Dakota (SD). Yup, South Dakota, "Home of the Coyote." To this day, I can't believe that I went to school way out in the Mid-West, not to mention it was my first time out of Florida, first of many times on a plane, and it was also my first time seeing snow. Funny, but prior to this time, I had no clue where South Dakota was except that it was located in the Mid-West. I finally took the liberty of looking it up for a friend on the map and the location made my mouth drop in mere bewilderment!

The first night in my dorm room was quite an experience because I didn't know how to turn the AC unit off. I froze like a county jail inmate with nothing to keep me warm due to the fact that my luggage, which had my comforter and pillow, hadn't arrive with me on the flight.

Ian, my roommate, was from Minnesota and was the coolest white boy I ever met. He had a huge Tupac collection and smoked a lot of weed, so we clicked up pretty good. I never had the urge or access to as much marijuana as Ian had showed me. There was an incident in the room within the first couple of days being roommates. His friend Steven came to our room and sat on my bed putting his sandals on my sheets. Where I'm from that's a no-no, but they couldn't understand why that was a form of disrespect. He acted as if I was joking when I asked him to remove his feet from my bed, but I did it with a smile to calm the situation. Maybe I shouldn't have done that, but I've never had a problem being rude to jerks.

In college at the professional track & field level, there are two seasons: Outdoor - in the spring and Indoor - in the winter. Nothing like winter season back home where we wore sandals and shorts, but up there, it was two pairs of socks, wool gloves, and snow boots.

I ran track with some of the fastest athletes in the Mid-West and most of them were white. Nonetheless, going to college meant a lot to me; I was living a dream. I picked up my game intellectually in the classroom, but physically I couldn't adapt to the freezing conditions to advance as an athlete; 20 degrees below temperature was common. However, I did win the first 400 meters race that season with no problem even though I came in as the underdog. Everybody was surprised, including me!

It was a disappointing season for me because I didn't excel to the next level as I had before since running in middle school. In college sports, it's either put up or shut up. In the classroom I was determined to be a scholar. I originally wanted to go to IU (Indiana University) for their business program since they were ranked number two in the country and their football program would be easy for me to jump into because their team was mediocre. The problem was that my SAT scores were not high enough to transition from high school to the college of my choice so the game plan was to attend South

The Courage To Believe

Dakota for a year, then transfer. In order to do this, I had to finish with a G.P.A. (grade point average) of 3.0 or higher. I earned an amazing 3.35 and impressed myself as well as everybody back home. I've never had those kinds of grades in my entire life!

Besides my ghetto-with-class style, I felt a culture shock being around so many white people. I was homesick without a ghetto around, especially without my Beautiful Black Women (BBW). Ever since I've had a taste for women, I've admired a woman's body, (truly a work of art) as well as their hearts and minds. The lips, the curves, the breasts, the thighs, the touch, the feel, the aroma of these beautiful creations of God will always be appreciated by gentlemen. In addition, when these women are beautiful on the inside, they are invaluable.

Without a doubt, women were on my mind, but there were none on campus cut from the fabric of my preference to be a distraction. I was isolated in South Dakota—an outsider. The transfer students from Sudan, Africa must have felt like outer space aliens even more so. I had a bias against them because they didn't consider us black people from America to be Africans. They were the true "Africans" which got under my skin, I must admit. There were a group of about six Sudanese exchange students, all having these facial scars that were initially hideous to me. Each of their foreheads was marked with two to three long, horizontal, raised welts. The marks on their foreheads were tribal marks.

One day I ended up sitting next to them in the dining hall, and with my bias in place, I was dumbfounded when they spoke to me. It was perfect English with no accent whatsoever. I introduced myself and eventually they explained the tribal marks on their forehead. From that day forth, those hideous scars became beauty marks to me.

The schoolwork wasn't a walk in the park either. College Algebra wasn't easy by a long shot, but with the help of the university math department-tutoring program, I made it look like a piece of cake. I got so good in the subject that I corrected the professor on a test problem that helped everyone gain seven extra points; a few students passed the test because of the boost and ultimately passed the class. Before I argued my case, I showed my tutor Elizabeth the test problem. She thought I got it wrong too at first, but I was convinced that I was right according to an algebra rule that she taught me herself. Elizabeth wouldn't end our sessions unless she felt that I understood EVERYTHING that we reviewed. The light bulb went off in her head and she realized that I was right. Everyone in the class was clapping and cheering with my discovery. This was the pinnacle of my college career. I ended up with a B+ as my final grade. I remembered the feeling of success I had in Mrs. Wyche's fifth grade class and I knew that the feeling of accomplishment is an addiction worth feeding.

Other courses that I excelled in were History and Poetry. I've always loved history, except for American history because America's story is comprised of the same old topics of Colonialism and Civil Rights violations or the lack of the latter. The history of this great country is full of founding fathers that met on Capitol Hill to write contradictory laws espousing freedom and "justice for all" yet all the while enslaving people

The Courage To Believe

by the thousands on their own properties ... listing men, women, and children on chattel ledgers like so many livestock. My forte was more in the ancient history ... about the history of the Caribbean, the Mayan Indians, the Warrior Kings & Queens of Africa, the world domination plots of Phillip and his son. I became stronger learning about historical characters like Shacka Zulu and Alexander the Great.

I loved going to history class high because it made me visualize better what the professors were explaining. It was my form of entertainment; the only bad part was that I often couldn't read my notes too well.

My poetry class really taught me how to describe my feelings, thoughts, and passions on paper. I also got a revelation of how ghetto my writing was. I was so embarrassed when the professor made all those corrections on my first essay. I could see all the red markings on my paper before she laid it on my desk. Ms. Kulligan, the professor, had us sit outside in the fall to breathe in the fresh air as we wrote our poems. She wanted us to capture the beauty of the orange and red leaves falling from the trees while the squirrels were mating.

The poem below expressed my feelings during my first time away from home. It's called "Reverse" and was published in a 2000 book of poems.

Reverse

As I sit on this crate
The thought of my escape
Won't go away.
Just last year I was in
Tears, now
I'm full as a tick with bears.
Being who I am isn't easy,
I'm one in a billion and knowing
What I know makes me even
More unique—
One in a trillion,
A Floridian in Vermillion.
Changes come and
Flames go.
Like a wild horse begging
You to see what is wrong before
He gallops away into the mid-west,
Searching for a better day.

"Reverse" illustrated my life leading up to my freshmen year in college. Education wasn't the only thing on my mind. I enjoyed the college life a little, but I must admit I wasn't trying to enjoy every vice that my peers were indulging in. Hard work goes a long way and then it's time to play.

The college parties were really crazy. These people knew how to drink and they passed the skill on to me. There were many nights when I got really tore up. I would've never thought that drinking beers could get a brother so toasted. I

The Courage To Believe

always thought of beer as a white man's high and hard liquor as the black man's because we needed to drink our problems away. I learned how to mix drinks and mingle the Midwestern way. It was a *Different World* and I enjoyed it. I finally found out what a keg was. My boy Russ, a white class mate, looked like one of my favorite actors Robin Williams and was the fastest person I ever ran with. Well, at least one of them. Russ use to make this drink called "Frog Juice," sounds yucky but it was actually really good. It was made from chopped ice with Mountain Dew and Vodka mixed in a blender. It comes out with a nice lime green color and creeps up on you.

No matter how hard I partied, I would not go anywhere without completing 60 to 100 percent of my homework/projects on any given night. Growing up, we were raised to finish our work first before we were able to play outside or play our Atari. When I was around nine or ten years old in elementary school, mom wouldn't let me ride my red BMX bike she bought for my 10th birthday until all my homework was done.

Watching my fellow Coyotes drink away their tuition made me focus: business before pleasure. Also, my long distance relationship with Sarah forced me to let off my frustration in academics; I am glad that my hormones chose the books, and not sex and drugs … the perfect example of making the best of a bad situation.

My relationship with Sarah went from a walk in the park to a rollercoaster. The reason for that was because of my confession to her. The secret was about an escapade that I had with my ex, Queta. Before I left home for South Dakota, I was working in a warehouse and on every lunch break I would call her on a pay phone due to the fact that I was as "broke as a joke." On top of that, my home didn't have a phone. Every time I would use my .35 cents to call Sarah, she would say that she was busy doing someone's hair, but she knew that the pay phone was my only form of communication other than dropping by in person, which was limited. If she missed me or wanted to talk for three minutes, she could've interrupted her weave sessions to speak to me. I understand the principle of business before pleasure, but we didn't have time on our side.

It seemed to me that since we were leaving for college, Sarah to Tallahassee, FL and me to Vermillion, SD, that she was pushing me away. After two weeks of not seeing her or even a five minute conversation, Queta stopped by right on time wearing this skin tight red skirt with two gifts. She never dressed like that. One of the gifts was wrapped in giftwrap and the other was wrapped in a G-string. My flight was in 24 hours and all I could think of, other than missing my family and few friends was that I didn't have any "chocolate" before leaving home. The flesh was weak, and she was looking so fine. Besides, she cried because I was leaving and thought that we would never see each other again. I could never bear to see a female cry. I gave in...

Back to Sarah - I felt so guilty about my weak moment with Queta not to mention, my conscience was eating me alive when Sarah told me that she didn't know how to say good-bye. Therefore, *months later*, I confessed what happened between Queta and me; mainly because my conscience was devouring me. If I didn't tell her, she would've never known; I just didn't want to continue our relationship without being honest. I had too much respect for her. She forgave me and we jumped over that hurdle together and Lord knows there would be plenty of others. Around that time, Ron McDougle and his roommate Terrell (black athletes from Florida) kept making remarks about "my girl."

Terrell commented, "I wonder what your girl doing now in Tallahassee."

"It would be a shame if I was to knock you out over something so childish." I told him. That was his warning and like a moron, he laughed.

Obviously, he didn't take my warning seriously because a couple of days later, he left a message on my answering machine about my girl again. All I can remember is that I snapped and dropped my book bag with a beat down on my mind even though he was a bigger guy than me. Before I left my dorm, I wanted to make sure Terrell was in his room so I called Terrell's room asking for Ron, but I knew Ron was in study hall and Terrell answered. It was already a long day and it just got dark outside while I ran across campus towards his dorm. Eventually, I realized that if I didn't slow down, I wouldn't have the energy to put my foot where the sun didn't shine.

I got to the dorm and took the stairs to his floor-the third floor. The freaking hall door was locked so I banged on it until someone came and opened it. Terrell's door was unlocked and he was laying down looking so cozy while watching, "*A Different World.*" I told him to get up very calmly because I wanted him to have a chance to defend himself. He knew what time it was so he got up and I knocked him right back down with a mean right. Boom! Then, I jabbed him with a left chased by another big, right hook. After a couple of hits, he grabbed me and screamed for help. He was so lucky that someone across the hall heard the racket and pulled me off of him. I probably would've beaten him until he was unconscious. I was pissed that I didn't get a chance to finish his whooping, but he got the message loud and clear.

Irrationality was my middle name. Even though it felt good splitting that prick, it wasn't worth being kicked out of school only to be sent home empty-handed. He could go back to being the poster boy for Jerks R Us while I got back to the books. Besides, Big Momma wasn't having any parts of me being expelled from school, especially after all the bragging she was doing about her second child in college. Luckily that wasn't the case. I finished the spring semester, my last semester at USD, without a hitch. My boy Lee, from Dominica, was going to Omaha, Nebraska every other weekend and told me I should vacation for the weekend at his mom's house while all the drama from the fight cooled down. I am forever indebted to his mother, Ms. Serrant, who became my second mother. His family has showered me with amazing kindness over the years.

ELEVEN

GROWN MAN STATUS

Never in a million years would I've guessed that Nebraska had a huge black population, in Omaha, that was as ghetto as my hometown. The same drug hustling took place out there, especially on the 1st and 15th of every month. Trash on the streets, pot holes, and pairs of shoes hanging off of the power lines ... no doubt about it, I was in the hood. They struggled with the same issues that were going on all over the country in every low-income community. During Thanksgiving dinner, we ate at an historic community center. Even though this was my first Thanksgiving in the freezing cold, the warmth of the food filled my soul. Everything was marvelous, starting with the delicious turkey, sweet corn bread, meatloaf, roast chicken, collard greens, eggnog ... the works! It was tradition for the black families to have a second dinner at the center after eating at home. Lee introduced me to his friends that came back home for the holiday. We played a few card games while others played dominoes and spades (I had only played spades twice in my life.) The history of Omaha and how the tradition of eating at the center began was shared with me by some of the retired men there. An old man mentioned that there was a video tape he wanted us all to watch. The video was a documentary about the Red Summer riot in Omaha, Nebraska in 1919. This was a difficult time in America ... lack of jobs, racism, and not to mention, the brutal summer heat.

There was a riot after Will Brown, a black man, was accused of assaulting a white woman. Afterward, a mob of white men ransacked the downtown area of Omaha, looting guns and bullets. We are all familiar with race riots in American history, but what caught my attention was the fact that the angry white mob kicked their way into the courthouse where the alleged attacker, Will Brown, was imprisoned and unloaded tons of bullets into him while he burned, having been set on fire. This was the most gruesome picture I had ever seen. At the white woman's deathbed decades later, she confessed to lying about the whole incident. Better late than never, I guess.

If think that's something, lookup "Black Wall Street," where a whole town of black folks in Tulsa, Oklahoma were burned down by racist white folks because they were too successful. 3,000 African Americans died and over 600 black owned successful businesses lost. Among these were 21 churches, 21 restaurants, 30 grocery stores and two movie theaters, plus a hospital, a bank, a post office, libraries, schools, law offices, a half dozen private airplanes and even a bus system. The largest riot in American history, and the schools failed to teach us this, or the fact that our ancestors in Africa built the world's first civilizations. The question is why? I'll tell you why – knowing your history is power! Not knowing your history means that you'll lack the necessary power in recognizing the greatness that is within you. I owe this revolution of thinking to Malcolm X.

Even though I loved the history lessons, my main purpose in visiting Lee's family was to eat some really good food and to meet some ladies at a nice urban club located

The Courage To Believe

downtown in the area where the riots took place 81 years prior. Finally, Omaha exposed me to beautiful black women (lots of them) with my skin color, wearing skintight jeans and gorgeous dresses packed with big booties. Weave everywhere, voluptuous assets, and twists in their walks. I was in love and I felt right at home. Freshly smitten, and in love with silky, smooth chocolate; in town the shelves were more stocked than I had ever seen before. According to my brother's ID, I was 23; and I was fashioned in business casual attire- Cotton Club vibe.

Now South Dakota's college campus had a small, black male student population, and an even smaller black female population. There was a ratio of one black female for every 10 black males; the problem was that there were only twenty black males. The white girls up there were nice, but their backsides were flat, for the most part. It's a theory of mine that women's bodies adapt to what men prefer. In my opinion, men in the north like breasts and nice legs, and men like me, from the south like booty and thighs. I was craving for a strip club like the ones that we have back home: *Take One, Flavors, Mint,* and *Synn Citi* to name a few. I was much older now than the younger version of myself who used to sneak into strip clubs. While in junior high, we used to sneak a peek at the naked women on stage before we would get chased out by the security guards.

Going back to Florida was inevitable since I wasn't going to sign up for another student loan. It has to be illegal the way these financial intuitions make thousands of dollars in loans so easily accessible to irresponsible college students. It would be just a matter of time before I would have to leave college unless, by some miracle, I decided to make South Dakota my home. That would've been an excellent choice for my career, being that I found intellectual success there, an experience that I was reacquainted with during my last semester leading up to my graduation.

I was sad to leave a handful of individuals that were true friends. I used to say, "A best friend is a dead friend," but after my experience with USD, I knew that there were still some genuinely nice people in the world. Unfortunately, they were and still are the ones who get taken advantage of.

Ultimately, I got the G.P.A. that I was striving for and had the opportunity to transfer to Indiana University. However, not being able to excel in Track & Field that year hindered my chances of receiving a full scholarship. Even though the relocation to IU did not take place, it was a victory nonetheless. By reaching for the moon, the stars were in my possession.

No one was pleased about me coming back home to continue my education, especially Mom. She knew that I would hang around the same friends I was drinking and smoking with before I headed off to South Dakota. Florida Atlantic University was my next destination and at the time, FAU (whose mascot is The Owls) had this second-class aura. That changed after they concluded a pretty good football season with a legendary coach who came out of retirement from the University of Miami, Coach Howard Schnellenberger. He led UM to a national championship defeating Nebraska in 1983. It was time for me to get back on the football field to finish what I started in high school, but before that could happen, I had to get my ducks in a row, so football was placed on hold.

In time, things would change drastically in my life affecting my graduation goal. In the fall of 2000, I began my journey at FAU as a marketing major and was doing pretty well for a 20-year old. I had a good summer full-time job working on beautiful yachts, prepping boats before they were painted. Working on those gorgeous vessels gave me the taste to acquire one. These boats would cost the owners an average of $250,000 just to repaint or to restore the wood finishes. Every client was either a millionaire or a multi-millionaire. There aren't too many people with a quarter of a million dollars at their disposal.

Mom begged me to stop working there because she was tired of me coming back home looking like a white ghost from all the sanding down of the boats' old paint and wood. I was a mess every day and dog tired; the skin on the palms of my hands was worn, very tender. The sanding made them extremely sensitive to the slightest touch. The pay was really good for a young man making $500 a week, but the owner of the business started playing games with my pay, so I quit. Two weeks after my departure from that gig, *Zales® Jew*elry called me in for a sales opportunity. They were pleased by the way I presented myself when I turned in my application. I was dressed professionally with a nice haircut and smelled great as well. Zales sounds and looks good, but it's just the name because the pay was just above minimum wage, plus commission.

I remember saying to myself, "I wouldn't switch my life with anyone for anything in the world." I had a savings account, I was in college, and had girls at my beck and call. At some point during this period, my Auntie Isna became terminally ill. I was so busy with work, school, and hanging out with my friends that I didn't bother to visit her in the hospital. All my other relatives were visiting her as her condition worsened, so eventually I went. The doctors couldn't figure out what was wrong with her, therefore, they couldn't help her at all. As a result and feeling it would be better for her, my family requested that she spend her last days at home with family rather than expire slowly in a cold hospital. Her body weight dropped drastically and her hair was so thin. My auntie was a sweet woman that never allowed a curse word out of her mouth.

To see her in the condition she was in was hard and left me with a sharp pain in my stomach. It always amazed me that the sweetest people are the ones that always get the short end of the stick. The doctors in the states and in Haiti never determined her illness. The suspicion that someone put voodoo on her filled the air, but that was just a rumor since she didn't have any known enemies. She passed away less than a week after I visited her in Little Haiti (Miami, FL) and I took a guilt trip for a couple of months. Of course, I knew that I couldn't save her, but it's the fact that I didn't have my priorities in order. Family first, no matter what! Losing her was one thing, but the guilt of not seeing her was even worse. Auntie Isna and I weren't that close, but I began to get closer with her younger sister, my Auntie Lolo, as a result of her passing.

The Courage To Believe

Two weeks after Auntie Isna's death, I went through another episode—the coin flipped. Already tipsy and not in a rational state of mind, I went to a club with a few of my friends. Drunk, sky high, and acting foolishly, we ended up getting into an altercation with a couple of dudes. Words were exchanged and those guys left the area of the club where we were, but not for long. Two of the dudes returned with reinforcements and jumped us. I got hit first with a bottle across the middle of my face. Blinded instantly by the blood pouring over my eyes, I just kept swinging, and another bottle hit me on top of my head. Another one of my homeboys had to get staples on the back of his head from a bottle wound. I returned home immediately, around 2:00 a.m., and my sister started to cry after seeing me all bloody. She convinced me to go to the hospital, so we went together. The doctors suggested that I get stitches, but I wasn't having that. The inevitable scar was bad enough and stitches were not going to happen due to the fact that I've seen stitches on people's faces before. They only seem to punctuate the wound and guarantee a nasty scar, drawing attention to it like the shiny zipper around an open fly. Years later, the choice not to get stitches would prove to have been the right choice because my skin healed favorably. . I was left with an obvious scar under my left eye. As handsome as I was and still am, it took me about a year to get used to, but like a soldier, I kept moving forward.

Five guys were with me and only two of us were fighting. It didn't make sense to me and I knew that an evaluation of my friends and life was necessary. With the death of my auntie, financial issues, and a scar on my face that needed to heal, I dropped out of college with every intention of coming back after a semester. It just seemed right at the time, especially with the immense amount of stress, not to mention my substantial slip in grades.

In life, I learned that sometimes you've just got to step back and analyze what's going on rather than continue forward fumbling without a good grip on the real world. In my case, I didn't have a grip on reality. And the reality was that I was losing in life—big time. What made it surreal was that I was just on top of the world just a few weeks prior.

The next thing I did was change my location less than a month later. After my 21st birthday, I got a townhouse out west in Fort Lauderdale with a childhood friend, Mike Robertson. We knew each other since the sixth grade and remained friends throughout many years. The townhouse was beautiful, with two rooms and two and a half bathrooms, stairs and a pool that changed to indigo blue under the moon. The place was furnished with Mike's things from his previous apartment and I was never comfortable with that. As a man, I felt that something in the place should've been owned by me. All the furnishings including the dishes, cups, glasses … all his. The issue was brought to his attention but, he just laughed and told me, "Don't worry about it; what's mines is yours." A problem was inevitable, sooner or later. I was on his territory and should have been more proactive, but because he was labeled as a friend, I let my guard down.

Nonetheless, the problem came after about three weeks of moving in. I began dating an older woman, a 28-year-old black woman named Neisha, who happened to be an ex-Marine.

The Courage To Believe

She was the definition of a complete woman; a single mother of two, educated, extremely attractive, and a superb cook. Every weekend for a month, she would come over with her niece Kim, Mike's girlfriend. Neisha loved to cook as much as I loved to eat so we were a perfect, sexy couple. Neisha was a grown woman with a great job as a manager at Microsoft's® corporate office, so money was never an issue. She taught me a lot about dealing with women—classy women; the first female to show me, other than my mother, what an independent woman was about. When it was all said and done, Neisha raised the bar of standards on what I wanted out of a relationship, which was to be served like a king, and how a woman should cater to her man. To top it all, she would roll-up blunts perfectly for me, however, she didn't smoke. She wanted to serve me in any and every way possible. She would spontaneously buy groceries to fill up my fridge, gave me "Lewinsky's" at the drop of a hat, cooked dinner and then fed it to me. All she wanted me to do was take her out every now and then, listen to her, and treat her like a lady. Being a lady's man of this sort was not a problem. She was an unbelievable woman and it was my pleasure to be her young lover.

Because she was an older woman, I learned a great deal about relationships and the pleasures of a real woman. We loved waking up with the birds chirping softly next to my window. It was very soothing after a long night of back breaking and sweating buckets of passion. We would do it while she was cooking since she enjoyed cooking naked or in just a G-string. Neisha definitely introduced me to the benefits of the adult birds and the bee's.

One afternoon, Neisha and I fell asleep on the couch and left a mess with the pillows out of place on the couch. Mike got upset about it because he always acted like "Mr. Clean" whenever his girlfriend was around for the weekend. It was an obvious front. During the week he lived like a pig. All his work clothes would be on his bedroom floor and every dish he ate from piled up in the kitchen sink until his girlfriend would come over on Friday nights, and then he would quickly clean them before she arrived. I was in the kitchen with Neisha when Mike said something about the pillows. All I said jokingly, was, "Now, you want to be Mr. Clean?" He said something underneath his breath. Neisha told me that I should not have said anything because I exposed him in front of his company, and she was right even though I meant it as a joke.

The whole week he ignored me by going straight into his room after picking up garbage all day at work (he was a career garbage man, but couldn't pick up the garbage in his house which was an ironic). We spoke about the "couch situation" like men and came to an understanding. There was no cursing or raising our voice involved in the discussion. The following weekend after the "Mr. Clean" incident, Kim didn't come through as usual, so Neisha came alone that Saturday evening. Mike came in with his two big, muscle bound uncles and his stepfather.

"Y'all step back outside while I talk to Kevin," he told them.

The Courage To Believe

I insisted on them staying and instead, Mike and I going outside to talk. Once outside, I saw a U-Haul® truck and realized what time it was.

Without a warning, Mike told me that he was moving out. The audacity of some people can be mind boggling, but why fight hyenas? I don't really remember what was being said on his part, but I do remember that he never looked me in the eyes the whole time. No advanced notice, no rent, and no friendship. I didn't know whether to knock him out or to shed a tear. I wasn't sad over the rent that needed to be paid (our first payment). I was feeling down because of all the years of knowing him and his family, he made the decision to be so conniving to a good friend. He owed more than to just spit on all those years of friendship. We played little league football against each other and played high school football together. I'm the one who got him and his girlfriend (also his baby mama) back together when they lost contact with each other after he got locked up and dropped out of school.

I just couldn't believe it, but I did accept it. It is what it is! I went back in to grab my car keys from my room and played a song from Tupac's *Until the End of Time* album, "Hate on Me." The song was perfect for the occasion since it was about a backstabbing friend. The timing was great so I played it as loud as possible on repeat with my room door open to make sure they could hear it as they packed up his stuff. Then I left to buy some pots and dishes for the kitchen since I had none of my own; they were all his. Yeah, I knew from then on to follow my instincts ... always have your own belongings in shared quarters. If you're paying for part of the Chinese

Checker Board, it is fitting for a grown man (or woman) to have his or her own marbles on the board. Also, no one can feel as if they hurt your ability to play the game when they decide to pick up their marbles and go.

The rent was $850 plus water and light. I worked full time at Zales® Jewelry in the Sawgrass Mall (one of the country's largest outlet malls), but had to pick up a second job to help pay the other expenses. I was planning on going back to school that summer, but the reality of working sixty hours a week made that dream impossible. Something had to give: school or work. Finding a roommate wasn't easy, but I needed one badly on the grounds that the money I was making was just enough to keep my nose above water; one false move and I would have drowned. The landlord being black made her a bit more lenient, and due to the fact she knew the situation with Mike.

Mike left some clothes and some miscellaneous things in the apartment, but wasn't able to get in since I changed the locks a few nights after he moved out. If he wanted the rest of his things, all he had to do was pay his half of the rent, which was only fair. He refused to pay his half and thought if he could break in that he wouldn't have to. Coming from work early one sunny afternoon, Mike was at my door waiting for me with his mom as his sidekick, but it turned out that he was waiting on a lock smith. As soon as I pulled up, Mike came charging at my car and kicked in the driver window. As his foot rose, I leaned towards the passenger side the best I could because I had my seat belt on. Shattered glass flew everywhere and a small piece jumped right into my left eye and dreadlocks.

The Courage To Believe

I shook off some of the glass, and put the car in reverse to back away from him as fast as I could get Ms. Dimes to maneuver ("Ms. Dimes" is what I called my 1985 Classic Box Chevy.) He got in the middle of the road talking junk, so I drove forward full speed to run him over. I barely missed. Thank God I did and sped off around the corner to get myself together. I took a crowbar from out of my trunk, but threw it down because my hands were good enough to give him a descent whooping. We squared off throwing fists at each other, and then I caught him with a punch to his throat that knocked him off his feet. He got up and tried to throw a handful of sand in my eyes, but missed. It was funny how once he got up he started jumping up and down like an orangutan making these weird noises. By this point, I knew he was crazy … perhaps missing a few marbles. I didn't know this guy. This wasn't the Mike I grew up with.

The lock smith and police arrived with the sirens screaming, so Mike took off running because he knew that he was going to get arrested which would automatically violate his probation. In case I forgot to mention, the townhouse was in a predominately white neighborhood near a lovely golf course. Here we are, two young black men bringing all this mayhem to their peaceful neighborhood. I know the neighbors were like, "Look at these negroes—there goes the neighborhood!" The officers asked me if I wanted to press charges, and out of anger I said, "Yes." The ambulance wanted to take care of my eyes since there was a piece of glass still stuck, but I knew that I would get charged a couple of hundred dollars. Since I had no insurance, I told them that I would take the glass out myself and I did. That may have been a silly choice, but I saved myself a couple hundred dollars and my eye. Thank God because I could've lost my eye trying to move the piece of glass with a Q-tip. Later, I reneged on pressing charges because his parents agreed to pay me the other half of the rent. The apple never falls too far from the tree. His parents never kept their word on the rent so it's no wonder Mike lacked honor. Besides, I didn't believe in using the law to handle my personal business. In the ghetto, we learned to obtain our own justice and to keep the white man out of it— a mindset that I once took pride in. I now frown upon my culture's ignorance.

Once all his furniture was out of the townhouse, I furnished it with my perfect credit. For the first time in my life, my sense of style was given the opportunity to express itself. I hooked up the place with mint leather green Natuzzi® couches, some paintings to compliment the furniture, a nice wood and chrome dining table with stylish chairs, and a king sized bedroom set with two swords over the head board. I was going for a contemporary style and the place never looked so good. The good taste comes from my mother who was known for her eloquent taste in clothes and furniture. If given the opportunity to have a substantial amount of finances, I will someday purchase pieces of furniture from old castles and palaces, along with artifacts. In fact, I plan on it.

By the time I found a roommate, or should I say a roommate found me, it was too late since I was already behind in my bills. Coincidently, my new roommate was named Mike but he was much older, cool, and extremely neat. We definitely shared one thing in common, which was smoking weed or "mint." Being Jamaican, he wouldn't smoke anything but the

The Courage To Believe

best. This dude was always sky high, but that's how he relaxed since he worked a lot of hours.

As mentioned before, the rent and other bills were backed up like crazy. Everything from credit cards, utilities, and the $850 a month was killing me mentally, physically, and financially. I was spiritually ill as well, since I wasn't going to church at the time and was only reading the "Word" sparingly. I'd make partial payments and hustle what I could hustle to make ends meet, but I was in a bad situation. Thank God for women because if it wasn't for Neisha making me smile and giving me that Lewinsky healing, I probably would've jumped off a bridge. I'm joking, but my situation at the time wasn't funny at all. Even years later just thinking about it makes me cringe and at times smile at my accomplishments because I've paid my dues.

The things we wouldn't have done if only we knew the end results of our decisions before we made them. Could you imagine the amount of money we would have saved or the amount of mistakes that would have never taken place? Six months on my own, and I was ready to go back home, but my pride wouldn't let me. If I were smart back then, I would've left the townhouse as soon as Mike moved out, and registered for school. Instead I began hustling dope for a financial boast. That wasn't fast enough cash. I needed more, so my friend Kenny came up with the idea of robbing a jewelry store by grabbing a couple pieces of diamond jewelry. Kenny was supposed to run up in there with no ski mask, and even though his face would be seen he wasn't going to make the news without using a gun or killing anybody, meanwhile I waited outside to drive. When we got to the store, he didn't want to go inside anymore and wanted me to go in there with him; I should've thrown in the towel then, but I was determined to complete the task at hand.

We parked the car in the ally and entered the plaza through a back alley. My adrenaline was pumping and I was noticeably shaking. I haven't done anything remotely close to this in a long time. Peacefully we walked in, and then placed the ski masks on our face in a little hallway near some payphone booths. We ran quickly into the store seeing just one customer inside with her little daughter. I grabbed a chair, broke a jewelry case, and took the most expensive pieces as quickly as I could, stuffing them in my pocket. Kenny took what he could. I took off first with Kenny following after me through the crowded hallway leading to the getaway car. The car belonged to a crack head that he supplied dope to. An undercover cop followed us outside with his gun pointing right at us, but knowing he couldn't shoot; we ignored him and sped off.

I can testify that having friends that aren't of a positive mindset can and will ultimately destroy you.

The cops had a blockade for five square miles, as soon as the store alarm went off. We got caught after putting them on a short speed chase. The traffic and rainy weather was no help.

This incident was the beginning of my criminal career. It's not that breaking the law was new to me, but now I just didn't care anymore. I figured that since I'll have this burglary case on my record (courts determined it to be a robbery since

The Courage To Believe

the store had occupants), my life was over as far as college goes because you must have a clean record to have a great corporate career. For the most part, this is true, but not the whole truth. I started doing things that I never thought I would be part of: drinking at bars, associating with prostitutes (best customers since they bring new clients), and selling crack … hanging out all times of the night, and many times while the sun was rising, I was still up. I can testify that having friends that aren't of a positive mindset can and will ultimately destroy you. My hopes, my dreams, my family to be, my whole world was fading away. Everything was going wrong for me, I mean everything. I soon gave in and sat down to eat at satan's table thinking that, because of my mistakes, I might as well run wild with the world. And that's exactly how the devil wants us to think because our thoughts activate our actions. The truth was that anyone could bounce back, but the demonic spirits work hard to keep us from knowing this by using tactics such as depression, lack of confidence, and guilt. All I knew was that I was heading nowhere fast.

TWELEVE

Lion's Den

In the Old Testament in the Bible, there is a story about Daniel, a man who was thrown into the lion's den for violating King Darius's law regarding prayers. Daniel knew that praying was against the law, but prayed anyway because spending time in the presence of God was essential to him. It was Daniel's faith in God that ultimately kept him unscathed while in the den. I knew in my heart that I made a mistake; I believed that God's grace and mercy was going to get me out of the mess that I somehow got into. This was my first time being locked up as an adult. It was quite the experience, but I felt a bit of relief from the pressures of life—of the world. Could you imagine having the love of being around thugs? We were all in the same boat. I didn't have to worry about anything that a "productive member of society" had to deal with; prime example of how foolish I became. We didn't have to pay any rent, water or light bills, no credit cards, gas, or taxes—absolutely no responsibility. The county took care of us. All we were responsible for was the washing of our underwear in the toilet. Arguments usually occurred if you washed them in the sink.

One more thing puzzled me; almost every dude had a tattoo of a naked lady on their arms, backs, or necks. Guess I didn't get the memo. On top of all that, the food they served us wasn't worth the cheap plastic brown trays they served it on. The food was horrible. Luckily for me I've never been a picky

The Courage To Believe

eater, as long as the food was good, I was eating it. In this case, the cuisine was disgraceful.

All the men behind bars had one thing in common: we all screwed up somewhere. I lost a lot of things while I was locked up -- my perfect credit, my townhouse, and most of all, my reputation. It's like once you're in the system, society and even your families turn their backs on you. I missed my cousin Duke's wedding, which was the day after my arrest. My charges were robbery without weapon, wearing a ski mask, fleeing, and resisting arrest without violence. My bail was $25,000 and my relatives were scrambling for the money due to all the expenses that were spent on the wedding. My sister, Kerlene, battled the hardest for me financially; she even had to fight off our other siblings from taking my possessions. I told her to sell my baby, my 1985 Box Chevy Classic called "Ms. Dimes" (when the car was purchased there were a lot of dimes between the sheets- I mean seats, *laughing out loud*); Kerlene wouldn't sell "Ms. Dimes" because she knew how much the horse meant to me. After about twenty days, I was bailed out and remained free for a time.

Instead of going back to being a "productive member of society" I began to sell crack full-time. I was already hustling a little here and there before, but not to the point where I ate, slept, and crapped crack. When I was at FAU, I had a money machine from selling weed to the students and custodians. A nice operation I must admit, but a hundred dollars a day wasn't enough for me when I knew I could be making a thousand.

Lion's Den

Dope dealing was a whole different level than weed. Both the risks and the costs went up…way up! People that smoke or sell crack don't sleep or *can't* sleep. I'd get calls 24/7 at all sorts of times in the heat of the night or middle of the day, and it didn't matter because it was about the greenbacks. I was as addicted to the money as they were to the drugs I was supplying them. As long as I was legit … it was on and popping. Without a car and a driver's license, a hustler is limited to the street corners, but if you have reliable transportation there are no limitations. I now had a 1987 Cutlass Supreme, which I drove everywhere it would take me; it was filled with gas, AC blowing, and speakers bumpin' Soulja Slim, 2pac, Shyne, and many other Gangster Rappers. If their music was real, I was feeling them. If I happened to have a lady in the car with me, I would play my old R&B classics like Barry White, Teddy Pendergrass, or Betty White.

Before my phone began jumping with delivery orders, I had to pay my dues on the street by standing on the corners. I chose to intentionally walk in order to find customers and give out samples along with my phone number even though I had a car. My goal was to get a feel for the faces and vibe of the streets. After a week or two, my phone was ringing consistently enough to hustle full-time. *No sleep* was the motto because the less sleep the more money. I felt like a walking zombie, rather, more like a driving zombie. All day and night, I was up and down the neighborhoods and interstates in the "Bat Mobile." In no time, the profits each day were $700 to a $1,000. The paranoia was intense from constantly looking over my shoulder for the police or the jack boys. Once in the drug trade, I was automatically enrolled into the "Any Thing Goes World," and a target for mistreatment of crooked police officers, the troubled spirits of the crack heads, and the jack boys who were plotting daily on taking my life and my money. Dope dealing opens doors to a lot of evil spirits that are better off padlocked shut. You can't trust *anybody* because everyone is looking out for themselves in the crack game. I wasn't even a key player ... but the more you hustled and sold, the greedier the villains became and paranoia was par for the course. I've heard of people killing their own family members over drugs or blood money.

On another note, learning how to cook cocaine into crack was interesting, just in the same way my history and science courses were simple. Who would've thought, in a million years, that I would follow in my Uncle Joe's footsteps and learn how to cook up cocaine? But by learning, I saved myself money. If not, I would have had to continue paying someone else to do it for me to the tune of $50 to $500 depending on the amount of cocaine being cooked, our relationship, and the experience of the chef.

Money was coming in and as fast as it came in, I was spending it. As a rule, where there is fast money, there are fast women in all shades, colors, and shapes. I never really had an issue of getting a date, but when I started selling dope, bigger were the backsides of the women that walked into my world. They were trophies on the streets. I bought a white, 1979 Cadillac Eldorado for about $2,000 using quick cash that I acquired from a *bank hustle* just the day before. Buying this car taught me the meaning of "chick magnet." Females of all ages suddenly were coming at me from every open nook and cranny, and they would do funny things just to get my attention. Needless to say, I enjoyed every moment of it. At least I had control of myself to ignore the teen groupies. The sad part was that I didn't have time to fornicate at every opportunity that *this world* presented to me. Business before pleasure may be an old principle, but I applied it to the third power. Nine, one of my top generals, and I would drive around as fresh as can be, competing on who could get the finest females from the strip clubs; he never liked dance clubs since the women required more effort. Of course, I would always win. Besides, he had a woman that he was in love with who took his time when he wasn't roaming the streets.

The Cadillac guzzled so much gas that if I wasn't a drug dealer, there was no way I would be able to afford to fill the tank on a daily basis; it had to be like $20 a day for gas costing $2.00 a gallon. The Big Caddy had its perks though. One female I caught with the Caddy gave Nine and me some Lewinsky while we were parked in a cemetery. I remember smoking a blunt and looking at the moon while she was handling business. It was creepy at first, especially since the street where the cemetery was located was called Elm Street. It was definitely disrespectful, I must admit, but it was exciting with the top down.

Nine showed me a lot of things from his perspectives which were interesting. My mom never really liked him, because his eyes were always red from smoking mint; his reputation didn't help his case either. Nine was what you would call a "Street Genius." We fed off of each other's ambition when it came to hustling. Robbery was a craft to him that he

The Courage To Believe

turned into a career. That was hard for me to understand at first, just like cooking and hustling crack was initially challenging. He even robbed a bank with a rifle while he was in middle school; one could only imagine how many capers he pulled! One thing for sure was that we were both "Action Junkies." It was routine for us to bust a "lick," then get high and drunk while we laughed about it afterwards.

You don't have to be in a grave to be dead.

Gradually, I was caught up in the green zone—all I could think about was money and more money. Death was what we were chasing when seeking that quick and irresistible wealth. We courted our destruction and flirted with our demise, all the while believing with each female conquered and each Benjamin counted, that we were winning. Everything seemed so easy and the temptations were rapidly flashing before my eyes. The Benzes, the Jag's, breaking off my family with bundles of money, the pounds of mint in bowls throughout the mansions so that my maids could roll them up, and strippers serving me was all I could think about. That's how the devil was playing with my mind. Push those high stacks of cash out the way and there was a tombstone with my name on it! You don't have to be in a grave to be dead. I thank God I had a spiritual foundation that never gave up on pulling me back to the light, back onto the right path.

Anything worth having in life is worth working for because no one can take it away from you once you've earned it. You could be dead or alive. I was dead alive. Once your spirit leans toward negativity like robbing and stealing, then you're already dead; it's just a matter of time before your flesh catches up with your spirit in the darkness.

At the time, I had no respect or order in my life. In the book of *Psalms 103:4*, it says that when people have no order, then disorder leads them to death or destruction. I was bent on taking and robbing; not contributing to the wellness of the community near or abroad. Hanging around Nine and some other dudes wasn't the best for me, and my mother knew it. I was so stuck on the fact that he was loyal. Despite his reputation (which he lived up to), he was a good friend. But learning how to rob stores placed my resume on another level. It took me in a direction of which I had no control. Once I ventured down that shady, dark road, anything was fair game. Like the old saying goes, "Birds of a feather flock together." I didn't love doing it, but I didn't hate it either. I felt like I was someone else, similar to how I imagined Popeye felt as he ate his spinach. Once the 9 mm gun was in my hands, I felt invincible and was pretty swift with it. I'm just glad no one tested my patience while the heat was in my steady hands. I remember my first lick like it was yesterday. Nine was far more experienced than I, and you would think he'd be the one with the gun, but it was me. Even though it was my first time doing an armed robbery, I was a smooth operator, as if I had done it plenty of times—one of those hidden talents that should've remained hidden.

Just like God gives talents to those who follow his commandments to enable us to save souls, satan will use those talents to do his work ... to do his will if the portal is open to him. He does it so that we will destroy lives—the lives of others as we wreak havoc on our own as well. The way I was living, the doors and windows were wide open to him and his demons. I was never nervous or panicked—a smooth criminal. After we robbed a restaurant, we went away to West Palm Beach and bought some Hennessy and a few bags of weed. We both agreed not to do any more adventures unless it was for six figures or better. So we went to the drawing board to figure out how we could safely get $100,000 or more.

It just so happened that we never got the chance to make any more moves because Nine was locked up for two years in 2002 and wasn't released until 2006 for an unrelated case. He went in the pen one month before I turned myself in for the burglary case. That summer, I tried to visit him at the Gun Club (Palm Beach County Jail) before they sent him to prison. The dress code didn't allow me to wear a wife beater, so I bought a shirt from someone in the parking lot for $5.00. He tried to charge me $10, but after speaking to him in Creole, he willingly obliged and sold it for $5. My Creole speaking isn't the best, but my comprehension has always been good. Heck, my English isn't even all that.

After doing all that, the guards still didn't let me in because the time limit everyone on the visiting list was given in order to check in was over. Sometimes, I felt as if I should've been the one to be caged up. We did the same things, if anything, I may have done worse. That dude was so crazy, so nonchalant, and certainly a loyal friend.

The day before sentencing for my robbery charge with Kenny (a friend), I caught a drug case —just my luck, huh? I pleaded no contest, but I should've taken the charge to trial. It wasn't a robbery. There was no gun and we didn't speak to anyone in the store, nor did we touch anyone. We were getting railroaded in the courtroom. At the time, I didn't know enough about the law, but I had money and should've used my finances for a lawyer. I rushed myself into a permanent criminal record. The sentence was eight months, with five years' probation and a hundred community service hours. The sentence was lenient for two reasons: one, it was my first offense as an adult and two, I took about $1,300 of saved drug money to pay for my classes before I stepped into the court room, knowing that the money would be refundable if I couldn't get into a classroom.

I knew that if the judge was to see proof of my school registration that it would show my intentions of going back to school as a positive weapon in court. The court appointed lawyer was only there as a front because his job was to get me to cop a plea, in doing so, he could collect the $700 the state of Florida was going to pay him. That's how they got the "The Circus" (system) set up with black males as the main attraction. I can hear their voices saying, "Go ahead, cop a plea so we won't have to worry about you in the future running for political office or working in a meaningful career." Stay in your hood, commit more crimes to make us more money, have more babies that grow up as bastards with their fathers caged up while your baby mommas' struggle their way into welfare. Tell your women that they are "bitches and hoes." Kill your brother, shoot your sister, don't read or learn your history, and sling crack so we can fill up these new jails and prisons. We are depending on you, my bro-tha, to fill up our pockets. We got prison contracts just waiting for you to get to work while we

The Courage To Believe

pay you .75 cents a day and we make $7,500 a day. Step right into the big top and join the greatest show on earth.

Judge Rothschild, a white-haired gentleman, wanted to give me a month to do what was needed to be done at home and then turn myself in. A month was too long, so I requested two weeks instead so I can hurry and make it in time for the spring semester once I was released. Besides, I didn't want to catch any more charges, which would add more time to my sentence. Those were the longest two weeks of my life. From then on, my routine was saving money and spending as much time as possible with my family and my new girl, Aries.

Aries had the most beautiful thighs and as much booty a man can handle. Her measurements were 36-24-36, and as fine as all out doors. She was the finest female I've had in my life since Neisha. A girl friend of mine, Shannon, introduced me to Aries since I was single and was going to need a female to keep me sane while on my county sponsored vacation. Since all of her friends I met weren't my type, I thought when Shannon called me to come outside that afternoon it would be another secret admirer. From the day our eyes touched, I told her, "I got to have you in my life." She smiled and told me where she was going to be in the next couple of hours and I was there wearing her favorite color—a blue Edgerrin James Colts Jersey, #34. To my surprise, she was just released earlier that day from prison after doing a year and a day ... long story.

Our first date was a romantic one. She wore this elegant pink dress with yellow flowers that was perfect for the summer season. I've always been a sucker for a woman in a dress. It was so late at night that I couldn't find a decent local restaurant, so we ate at Popeye's Chicken and went to the Las Olas movie theater in Downtown Ft. Lauderdale to see the movie "Unfaithful," starring Diane Lane and Richard Gere. The weather was perfect that summer night, so we took a walk along the docks and talked about our poems on the river front before entering the theaters. Aries had me wide open and she was feeling me too; both of us were wagging our tails. Telling her that I had less than two weeks to turn myself in would only ruin the night so I kept it to myself as we had a magnificent evening.

A few days later, Nine violated his probation by not making his monthly payments, so he didn't bother to report to his P.O. I did a lot of dirt with him, my partner in crime, but holding it down on my own was what I was made of ... a One Man Army. Every army has at least one ally, and Nine was mine. The state was willing to reinstate his probation, but he decided that he would rather go to prison. Reason being that he knew he would've violated his probation again because of his street lifestyle and constant smoking habit. That's definitely one difference between us. I'd rather be on probation with all of its stresses and pressures than to be incarcerated any day. On the outside, spring air, good food, and women were three of many reasons why being an inmate would never, ever, have been a deliberate choice. The appreciation of the simplicity in life was something that my mother instilled in all five of her children, no matter how much we veered off.

The day before I had to turn myself in was a Sunday in May of 2002. I packed up all my clothes and placed them in a garbage bag, hid all my money after giving my little brother Rube $500 for a rainy day. I gave my gun to one of my homeboys because gunplay wasn't his style and I trusted him. I started to miss every little thing about my house; the couch, the carpet, the grass, the mirror, the walls and the toilet stool. Similar to how it felt leaving Florida for South Dakota.

    Aries and I rented a room at a cheap motel, but it didn't matter because the lust was rich that night. We had weed, Alize, Hennessy, and one condom. We drank "Thug Passion" (a cocktail mix of Hennessy and Alizé) and watched an Animal Planet special on lions and hyenas. My homeboys stopped by to smoke a couple of joints with me and to wish me well, so the pleasure had to take a pause. Aries was drinking the Hennessy straight up as if it were Gatorade. Eventually, she passed out and I was disappointed, but after an hour she awoke only to throw up neatly in the toilet. She brushed her teeth and used some mouthwash and we were back at it. We made love for hours until four or five in the morning, sleeping for only two hours. She never had that type of energy; we were getting loose like it was our last day on earth. All she wanted to do was to make sure that I was fully pleased because we both knew that it was going to be our last time for a while.

THIRTEEN

THE BIG TOP

The next morning I sold my last pieces of crack to Tookie, a crack smoker, and then stopped by Mom's house to get a hug and a kiss. We were on bad terms at the time, but that morning it didn't matter. She was certainly disappointed, but she was still Mom and I was still her son. Aries and I went to IHOP and ate like kings. Not to mention I was three hours late for my appointment with the handcuffs. It was my last real meal. Did they really think I was going to be on time?

My head was held high as I turned myself in and it was going to be up just as high walking out. Eight months didn't seem long to me because all I was doing was praying, working out, and strategizing my future. My time wasn't wasted on worrying about what the next convict was doing. My mind and my heart were on my loved ones on the outside. I seldom made calls to my family because of the financial burden of the collect calls. Behind the jailhouse walls and barb wired fences the voices of your loved ones are priceless. They are the sound that deadens the madness of the cellblock, the sound that cushions the blow of loneliness, the sound that chirps hope like songbirds of freedom. Inside, the main thing is to maintain, no matter what. I figured as long as I can keep my head up and maintain my faith, then everything was going to be alright. Just let the storm settle.

The Courage To Believe

It was not unusual to have someone offer their whole food tray for a five minute three-way phone call —it was that serious. They were willing to starve 'til next chow (meal). The food was horrible; it was made up of generic substances that tasted like asphalt. For example, thick bologna, thick cheese, and salt-less rice made up our diet; the mere thought of the food made us all uptight at times.

Most of them had cases that were already stressful with ten to hundreds of years behind bars in their future. Some people had real problems to think about, ones they would have to face once they completed their sentences: baby mama drama, a load of debt and last, but not least, about who will take care of their children? Most men don't realize they are leaving their children to the wolves until they catch a case. It was rare to hear someone speak of their girlfriend or wife in a positive way. With the ones that did, you could see the love in their eyes, or maybe it was their desperation. Men always complain about how their women aren't trustworthy, but if the tables were turned, men would be cheating on their incarcerated women. We, in most cases, cheat on our women while we are free (not all men).

Mesho, one of my bunkies, told us a story about his first trip to prison. He was married to a ghetto fabulous female. She helped him hustle cocaine, ecstasy, and heroin up and down the city streets; they established a productive money machine. Now I've heard a lot of stories, but his was a true Bonnie and Clyde tale. They both were hustlers and made a lot of money. He got caught with an unspecified amount of drugs (ecstasy pills and heroin) and was sent to prison for about two years.

Their empire was put into her hands, but it was too big for one person, so he had his cousin join the operation. His cousin got involved with his wife and got her pregnant. The money stopped flowing, a block was put on the phone, and Mesho was left in the dark. Finally, his wife came to the pen to visit him, but the visit didn't last any more than a minute because he heard the rumors about his cousin's affair. As soon as he saw her big stomach, he spit in her face and threw their wedding ring in the prison yard. Wow!

Another story was one about a guy who was in an abusive relationship. According to a cell mate, Andre, he and his girlfriend were always hitting each other. She even ran him over once, and he now walks with a permanent limp. One morning as he was ironing his clothes preparing to go to work, they got into it.

"I snapped," said Andre, "And smacked her against the face with the hot iron!"

I didn't know this guy Andre, but I know wanted to hit him. Bustas like him came a dime a dozen. Not all of them were bad or evil, some just made a random mistake while for others, making mistakes was a lifestyle. Stories like these were often heard, but it taught me not to put all my trust in any female that didn't prove she was worthy.

Listening to these stories was pure entertainment for me and one of my favorite past times, however, my first love was working out. I remember my first day in the recreation area. All the other guys were big and cut up—truly shredded with muscles from pushups, sit-ups, and pull-ups... The funny thing

The Courage To Believe

is that I hadn't worked out in a year due to my drinking Ol' English, smoking mint and packs of Newports. At first I couldn't understand how some of the inmates were able to work out the whole time we were let out of our cages, which was for two hours, three times a day. We were kept in small, crowded spaces and it wasn't unusual to see another dude's private whether we wanted to or not. It was just that crowded.

Two hours before noon, and two hours before and after chow, was our recreation time. Our recreation time revolved around when chow was served. They feed us like animals in a zoo, which is exactly how most inmates acted. Isn't it sinister how the nicknames jail has acquired, whether it be a *pen* or a *cage,* are terms fitted for animals rather than men? As time went on, the realization of why inmates' worked-out so hard dawned on me; it was the best way available to relieve stress other than choking your chicken, in other words, masturbating. Guys took advantage of the privacy in the showers to play with themselves. Whenever I took my showers, I made sure to have my shower slides on because of the filth that was in the dirty showers. Those jokes about dropping the soap in jail (not sure about prison) aren't true, but I tried not to drop my soap since the shower floors were covered with pubic hairs, soap scum, and semen. If my soap fell on the shower floor I would leave it there, even if it were my last bar; they were the same size as the ones in hotels and the showers were individual small closet size showers.

Other convicts either played games like monopoly, checkers, or chess all day, gambling for potato chips, cookies, or money that was give from friends, family, and outside sources. Some of those who had the luxury of making collect calls did it three to four times a day. I stayed clear of the phones because to me it was poison to my spirit. There was always some bad news on the other end of the line. A few inmates either read books or simply watched T.V.

My daily routine was to eat breakfast at four in the morning (everyone was served that early). Second, I would sleep until lunch, which was served between 11 and 12. Third, I would work out for an hour. Fourth, I'd take a shower (alone). Fifth, I would do more sit-ups until chow because we were on lock down by that time. During chow is when our pre-opened mail was given to us, if any. My family showed me a lot of love by keeping in touch with me by pen and paper. Sixth, we would go to lock down again until chow hall was cleaned up. This was the time when I would read or write my letters, if any, because I would feel better once I had food in my stomach. Seventh, the guards would let us out again until 10 p.m. This was pretty much my routine.

There were a few things that really bothered me about being locked up: the freezing temperature, having to smell another man's feces, and the constant naked squats some guards have inmates do as punishment. No matter how hard I tried not to look, there was always the mistake of looking at the wrong place at the wrong time. Guys have to relieve themselves and the fact that we were in a small area with about 50 other inmates made it impossible to avoid seeing someone else's private parts. I couldn't stand it. That wasn't even the worse torture; the constant blasting of the AC at 50° degrees was the worst. If you couldn't afford to order a sweater, then most likely you would either freeze or have to steal one and get into a fight.

There were a total of six inmates in my cell. Every once in a while someone had to do the number two, which is understandable, but what bothered me and I'm sure everyone else in the cell as well, was when we were in lockdown and someone had to drop a couple bombs. It's embarrassing and humiliating. "Put some water on it," someone would always shout, which means to flush in between droppings. Sometimes it was me who had to do the number two, but when you got to go, you got to go. It was common courtesy to try and wait until we were out of lock down so that we could use the bathroom in private.

As inmates, we were subject to constant searches. It didn't matter what time or where the searches took place. The "shakedowns" is what the guards called the group searches where there would be about 20 guards flipping and searching through everything and anything in the cells. The sole purpose of these shake downs was to find contraband, such as illegal weapons, drugs, and nude pictures of our girlfriends or wives. If they found any of these things amongst the inmates, then that individual inmate would get written up. After a day or so, that inmate would be transferred to another location within the property or another facility for solitary confinement.

One of the facilities that I was transferred to was the Joseph V. Conte Facility (named after an officer that was killed during a jail escape). Deputy Joseph V. Conte was killed in the line of duty on July 11, 1979, while escorting prisoners from the

Broward Sheriff's Office County Jail to a medical office in Fort Lauderdale. This new facility was built in 1999 (the year I graduated high school). They had a drug program for people who used drugs and for those like me who, by acting like drug addicts, would get their time reduced. The counseling sessions forced all of us to look into our souls. The sad stories of how these men were molested, physically abused, and hooked on drugs were depressing. Once during one of our sessions, one of the guys told us that September 20, 2003 was the 15th anniversary of when his daughter disappeared (September 20, 1988). The coldness of the world hit me at that moment. Some people can be so cruel that it is almost unbelievable. It was necessary for them to speak about the pain of the past in order for them to forgive themselves, those that harmed them, and those that they have harmed. I'm confident that these group sessions (of about 20 men) were helpful to the ones that needed it. I was there to kill time. However, I always looked forward to closing the sessions with a powerful prayer from one of the volunteer counselors that headed the program.

On the flip side, I enjoyed a couple of things. We were able to get our clothes cleaned once every two days. We'd place our clothes into individual net bags, and by morning we would get our clothes. I always looked forward to the fresh scent. The other aspect I enjoyed in that hell hole was the talent of this inmate named Robert, who earned the nickname R. Kelly, the legendary R&B singer/songwriter. He was a real heroin addict, and we could also tell that he didn't have all his marbles. Despite all that, this man could sing like it was nobody's business, which is how he earned his name. When he wasn't chewing on a toothbrush (all addicts had an addictive habit and his was chewing), he would sing whatever song we requested for a pack of cookies or a phone call. I probably was the first to pay him with the cookies. The way the facility was constructed allowed everyone on the same floor to hear R. Kelly if he sang into the air duct. This guy was blessed with a talent and it was unfortunate that he was heading to prison for 30 years for assault with a deadly weapon.

Nonetheless, there was a need for my own self-evaluation. There were individuals that didn't need to be in my life, and on the other hand, there were individuals I did in my life. So I took a piece of paper and wrote a list of all the positive and negative influences in my world. The positive side was much shorter than the negative. My vacation at the new facility gave me time to think of all the stupid things I've done and the shame I've brought to my family. Some of the memories were funny, like the time I sold Ms. Dimes and then stole her back with "The Club" still on the steering wheel. Talk about a mission impossible, now that was an hilarious evening. Luckily, no one was on the road that night to get hurt during that adventure.

On a serious note, the reason I sold her was to get money to buy bigger guns (fully automatic rifles) for a money truck robbery with a couple of my associates. Richard planned the whole thing since he used to work for Dunbar Armored, but backed out the day before we were supposed to do it. We had a plan covering everything that was needed to make the heist happen from the stolen van down to the guns. Even though this was an inside job, I was willing to do it without him since the rest of us were still down for the mission. As anxious as we were, three people just weren't enough. Richard ignored my calls, but I wanted him to tell me face to face that he wasn't down, so I went to his home to confirm what I already knew deep down. He was definitely on my negative side of the list even though I should thank him because, with my luck, who knows what could have happened. We could have ended up dead or on a permanent prison visit, or better yet, maybe even living on an island sipping on rum piña coladas. One thing was for sure - it wasn't worth the risk. Having wisdom to determine the balance between risks and rewards are pivotal in life.

The thought kept crossing my mind that maybe leaving South Dakota was a bad move. Apparently it was, but I can only imagine where I would be today if I would've stayed up there isolated with the excellent grades I was receiving. There's no doubt I would've probably been on the covers of Black Enterprise magazine along with Oprah Winfrey instead of reading about her from behind cold, steel bars. It's not that I regret leaving South Dakota because everything happens for a reason, but one can't help but to imagine the possibilities. For some reason, God wanted me to undergo everything I was going through, and I wanted to survive to see what his grace was up to. There are some events in people's lives that are difficult to bounce back from. Not for me, I'm going to always stand again. This is my core constitution—to bounce back with a determination to be that successful black man who would return to help his community and get others to find freedom in their minds. History records that Tubman freed almost 300 slaves and of those she could not free, it was because she *could not* convince them they were slaves (Congress). The ghetto life has many strongholds, and the shame of it is that most of us don't even know or recognize the strongholds that are passed down from generation to generation: no education, procrastination, and lack of unity, to name a few. *"My people suffer for the lack of knowledge." Hosea 4:6* (NLT).

Education was the first listed on the positive side of my life evaluation since it has always worked well for me. I haven't played football for a couple of years, but I had my mind made up to join Florida Atlantic University's football team to see if I still had it. Also on my list was to continue to sit on the beach while listening to the ocean waves at night; doing this allowed me to contemplate various thoughts and relax my mind at the same time. The power of God's grace can be easily seen looking at the sparkling ocean.

FOURTEEN

WET FOOT – DRY FOOT

In 2002, two hundred Haitian immigrants came to the Miami shores one afternoon in an over-packed boat. There was a nearby road they frantically ran towards and some hopped on the trucks that were passing by. All of this was captured live with news helicopters. I was sleeping in my cell until one of my homeboys, Black, called me out to watch what was happening on the news. Everyone came close to this small television to look at my people jump helplessly out of the boat into the water, as if they were leaping for freedom.

Ninety percent of the inmates were black and half of us were Haitians. What surprised me was that the black Americans weren't laughing or cracking jokes on Haitians as usual. The event touched everyone because of the desperate situation of our people. We all knew that they would be sent back to Haiti when it was all said and done. Within the next 48 hours, a boatload of Cubans came and they were welcomed to Florida with a parade and visas. This same routine continued for years later. America, the land of the free, where democracy is often a sad joke and the whole world knows it. How could the Bush Administration treat one race of people with a "Red Carpet," but treat another like garbage? I am so thankful that we have a new executive officer in President Barack Obama. (In 2008, he and his cabinet inherited a ran-down economy and a lot of work to be done, but it can and will be done.)

From that day on, I decided that once I had a chance to resume my education ... once I stepped foot on campus, my major would be changed from marketing to political science. The obstacles of getting into politics with a criminal background crossed my mind; I envisioned me running for political office and being persecuted by the media as they fired off my past like bullets to shoot down my chances for victory.

A change needed to be made with the immigration laws, especially the biased ones against Haitians. Maybe I was a bit emotional, but I knew something had to be done - we all knew it. Here in Florida, you hear a lot about America's immigration policies with Cubans vis-à-vis Haitians. We're so close to both islands. When Haitians come ashore, it is understood that they will likely be housed at the Chrome Detention Center where illegal immigrants in South Florida are sent. After a lengthy process, they are sent back to Haiti. In the case of Cubans, if the Coast Guard catches them in the ocean, before coming ashore, they are subject for repatriation. But here's the rub: if a Cuban immigrant actually makes it far enough for one foot to touch the shore, they can stay here in America while Haitians can have both feet on sand and roll around on the beach only to be repatriated. This policy is called "Wet Foot/Dry Foot." Maybe it would be more accurate to call this policy *Wet Foot/Dry Foot—White Foot/Black Foot.*

The American government has been spitting in our faces for decades, better yet, centuries. Toussaint L'Ouverture's movement of freedom destroyed France's institution of slavery along with the world social view and conventional thinking that blacks were inferior. From George Washington to the burning bushes, the United States envied Haiti for delivering the world's first major blow against slavery when General Toussaint, along with his two lieutenants Jean-Jacques Dessalines gave Napoleon a miraculous defeat (Heinl).

Back to reality — in jail, the abundance of drama was common. One of the most depressing moments was when Aries revealed to me in a letter that she was molested by her father throughout her childhood. It has always saddened me to think about that particular subject before I even met her, and she was the second female to share this awful experience with me. Incarceration isn't the best place to hear that type of news. Aries had not spoken to or seen her father in over a decade because she couldn't even stand to think of him. Not surprisingly, he just happened to be in prison for sexual assault.

The first female that told me about her violated past was Sandra, a girlfriend of mine while I was in high school. We were very open (a little too open) with each other and talked about everything … our triumphs, our failures, and our nightmares. Her uncle molested her several times when she was between the ages of seven and ten, while he was living with her parents. Out of fear, she never told anyone, but her older cousin caught him in the act. When her father found out that his brother had molested his daughter, it drove him mad. He didn't kill him, fight him or press charges, but simply kicked him out of their house. The family had a meeting and decided to let bygones be bygones. The whole thing was swept under the rug as a family secret due to her family's high status in the community. In other words, he didn't want to tarnish the family name which was straight up bull-S*@#!

The Courage To Believe

Back to Aries ... the real reason she told me her secret was because she felt that I should know, since she was in love with me and probably because she wanted me to accept her past, which was admirable of her. Not to mention that she was pregnant by me, this was the best news during my vacation. I guess the night before I turned myself in, that one condom just wasn't enough for our last night of passion. Our bond grew closer from that very moment on. If there was any doubt of my love and devotion to her, it was gone. She came to visit me many times, but the one that stood out the most was the one I asked her to lift up her shirt so that I could see her stomach. At that time, she was three months, and I wished I could have touched her belly. Me ... a father, yeah right, but it was very much real. The excitement filled my soul with a hope that was unexplainable. I remember looking at Aries and noticing how beautiful she was at that moment. It was as if she blossomed from a cute caterpillar into a butterfly. It's true that women increase in beauty while pregnant.

Shortly after, my high was demolished. She had a miscarriage after four months and it crushed me. I wanted to die, literally. It was God's will and I forced myself to accept what wasn't in my power to change. All my life, prior to that day, I had a couple of close calls, but this time was the closest and I was truly ready to become a father. I wasn't enthusiastic about Aries being the mother of my child, but having a child period is a blessing, but unfortunately it just wasn't meant for me as of yet.

As if that wasn't enough drama, my lawyer refused to visit me to discuss my drug possession case in Palm Beach.

I've heard of all the rumors about lawyers being sharks and crooks, but I experienced it firsthand. My attorney agreed on a two thousand dollar fee to plea out the case, which was a mistake in the first place; one thousand dollars before I turn myself in, five hundred dollars while I was incarcerated and the remaining five hundred when I got out. That was the deal. He tried to pressure my family to give him the remaining $500 while I was still in jail, which was not in our contract. My bunkies (cellmates) showed me how to fight back against the lawyer by writing a letter to him requesting a visit or by writing a complaint to the Florida Bar. I also learned that the jailhouse will notarize any legal letters that inmates write. Less than a week later, I got a visit from him. It worked like a charm. Slapping this S.O.B. would've been too easy albeit a stupid move. So, I hurt him, or should I say pinched him where it hurts—his pockets. I jumped out and didn't pay him zilch. He argued with me to plea out the possession charge even though I wanted to fight it. If only I would've gone with my gut feeling because I really didn't have a clue how much this one case would hinder my future: I wouldn't be able to vote, couldn't get a real estate license, and couldn't get a gun license to protect my home. Florida Law allows any felon to seal their record as long as there's only one felony on record. The drug case gave me two felonies, excluding me from sealing my record. This is one crucial mistake a lot of people that look like me make because we try to use our "get out of jail free" card to jump out too quick, instead of being patient enough to fight the charge. The system was created so black folks would bear the burden of the jails and prisons. Bottom-line is that I paid this attorney to do something when I could have pleaded guilty

The Courage To Believe

myself, for free. The way the whole thing unraveled never sat well with me.

This is how I caught the charge. I was driving home late one night from making a delivery to a client. While I was driving down a dark road, I noticed police lights behind me and I wasn't sure at that point if they were following me. I turned onto a street just to see their reaction and sure enough, they turned as well. At this point, I became nervous because I had some crumbs of dope in a super glue bottle which I was able to quickly put it in the crack of my butt; just enough so that I could hold the bottle by squeezing my booty muscles, and when I was ready to take it out, it was easily accessible. I knew I was 54 because I had everything with me from my registration, insurance, to my license. He was supposed to just pull me over and let me go with or without a ticket, after verifying my paperwork was legit. He followed me two miles to my mother's house and turned on his sirens. The officer asked me for my info which I gave to him, but my license was in my pocket.

"Where's your license?" The officer asks, "Get out the car."

I thought to myself, "If they would give me five seconds to look into my pocket, I would *produce* my license."

Just by the way he spoke to me, I knew it was going to be a long night judging by his attitude. I was guilty to him as soon as he turned on his sirens. I'm not even going to lie; the whole situation shook me once I realized the pig wasn't even going to give me a chance to look for my driver license. He opens the door and yanks me out. By this time there were four other white officers surrounding the car. The little bottle slipped out and fell down to the floor. I quickly reached for it and threw it as far as I could. They whooped my butt.

Mom, hearing the noise, gets out of bed in her night gown and steps outside into the heat of the night, only to be punched in the chest by one of the officers, causing her to fall. I then bowed one of them in the mouth and punched another one. I was immediately sprayed with mace, but I didn't even feel it until I was hog tied in the police station. The burning sensation from the mace was excruciating and I don't want to experience that ever again.

Once at the police station, one of the pigs saw my "Haiti" tattoo on my right arm carved in bold blue letters and shaded red in the middle. He kept making insults about my Haitian culture so I did the same about his Caucasian race.

The officer started making remarks like, "Go back to your county, you f***** n***, we don't need you Haitians here."

"You crossed-eyed paper cop, all you do is push paper clips," I shouted, "You're not even a real cop, get lost dude!"

He was cross-eyed so it was easy to insult him. It was so childish of both of us. After ignoring him for a while the situation cooled down, and I found the license in my pocket.

The Courage To Believe

Just my luck! If I were able to produce my license earlier, I wouldn't have a felony record today. They wouldn't have had the right to search me, so even if they did find something on me, which they did, the case would've been thrown out anyway. Due to my other felony (a withheld adjudication), I'm unable to seal or expunge my record. I know one thing, if I had money like Don King and slapped the right judge with $20,000, this problem would've disappeared - it's the American way.

That would have meant that I could be working in public office or in corporate America today. It bothers me, sometimes, thinking about the whole situation because a felony record would mean I'd have to be at the bottom of the food chain, or, at least that's what they thought. Everything happens for a reason is what I kept telling myself. A couple of days prior to this pounding I took from the police, I had a much more interesting adventure.

I was chilling in front of my homeboy's crib, wiping the windows of my '74 Eldorado Cadillac convertible. There was a substantial amount of crack hidden in the car (due to the fact others may be hiding important things in the same spot, I won't disclose the location). A red, four door car stops in the middle of the road and a short white dude jumped out in dress clothes, wearing a badge around his neck and with a shining chrome gun pointed at my head.

"Put your hands up!" the detective screams and I put both hands up with a Windex bottle in my right hand and cloth in my left.

I ask frantically, "What did I do man?"

The detective tells me, "We got a call that you match the description of a fugitive on America's Most Wanted." My mouth dropped.

"You got to be joking, America's Most Wanted!" I said in a sarcastic tone, "Do you think I'll be washing my car windows if I have a commercial on Most Wanted?"

He replied, "Shut the hell up, while I wait for backup. We're going to get to the bottom of this."

Once they found the drugs, I knew my bond would be revoked because I thought there was already a warrant out for stealing Ms. Dimes back. Backup arrived while he asked me for my name, address, and the usual jive so I gave him an a.k.a. The thing is I didn't have any ID, but I had a cell phone and two beepers (one was active) — the perfect description of a drug dealer, so they probably knew I wasn't squeaky clean. An officer took out a picture of the A. M. W. fugitive and they all agreed that we didn't look alike. Even though I didn't look like the fugitive, they were looking to stick me for *something*. They figured that I must have a warrant or was hiding something so the black female officer left to get the picture at the police station of whoever I said I was.

Meanwhile, I knew what time it was. Anyone caught with as much dope as I had would be locked up for more than three presidential terms. Quickly my brain devised a plan.

I told the officer, "There's my friend ... he could identify me," as soon as he turned his head to look, I took off like a mad man. With handcuffs behind my back, I jumped two gates that were up to my hips, almost falling on my face on the second fence. The heavy set cop couldn't keep up. I ran through a backyard that had a raging pit-bull in it, but my adrenaline overpowered my fear only to end up in another bushy area with my dread locks caught in the branches. I was stuck. They had the area blocked off anyway—quickly.

They took me into the precinct where I gave them my real name since my fingerprints were going to tell the truth anyway.

"Why did you run?" asked the officer that I tricked. "I'm black ... that's why," I replied. We both laughed.

The cop recognized my address because he was the one that came to my house when Ms. Dimes was reported stolen by the person I took her back from.

"I bet you ran because you thought we had an arrest warrant for the stolen Chevy," he said. I must admit he was pretty smart because of it.

I denied it, but he was right. However, to my surprise, no charges were ever filed. Every once in a while I think about how I was able to dodge that one. It was a pure blessing. The police got tired of searching my Cadillac because of all the rust under and between the seats—two blessings at the same time. All I had to do was sign a paper and they released me to the streets. I couldn't believe it.

As soon as I walked out, I looked up to the sky to thank God. They gave me back my cell phone, but my beeper had fell to the ground somewhere while I was running. I paid ten dollars to get it back from a little girl that found it in her back yard where the pit-bull was. And just like that, I was back on the grind. Isn't that something? I was definitely dirty enough to go to prison so, when I caught the charge for the crumbs, I couldn't complain at the time, but now that little felony is kicking my behind.

Now, back to my vacation…in my replacement, Ceebo, an ally was given my cell phone and my youngest brother Pharo was given my beeper. The purpose behind this was to make sure my mother's bills were getting paid and to have a little stash of cash waiting on me. Both of them let me down. Whether or not there was any deception is unknown; I was clear there was none, but my little brother was simply incompetent. When I got out the lion's den, my net worth was $40. At this point, that didn't matter to me due to the fact that I was free and ready for the world with big plans on the agenda.

Growing up I always knew there were two opposing institutions that could influence a person's path of life: school and prison. The threat of prison was the nightmare and schools were where dreams of success began. Now, as an adult, I realize I had a choice about which institution I wanted: a prison institution or an educational institution. Hands down, I chose the educational institution by devoting my time towards education and staying away from things or wrong choices of people, by any means necessary.

FIFTEEN

FOCUSED ON THE FUTURE

Mom was extremely happy to see me again and I was just as happy to hug her. At any given moment, she would pray or begin to shed tears of joy to see her young prince back home. Suddenly I remembered a random question she asked me one day.

"Kevin, do you love yourself?"

My reply was, "Yes, mom, of course I love myself."

At the time, I was too high to realize the seriousness of the question with my bloodshot eyes. The substance of the question never really hit me until I was locked up contemplating on the future with nothing but time to think about my choices.

Getting released from jail was like being born again. I went in as a reckless boy and walked out as a focused man. It was only eight months, but it was all I needed to get my life back. Within 24 hours on the streets, I caught the first southbound train smoking to Boca Raton and re-registered for school at Florida Atlantic University. There were all kinds of holds against me (late book fees, student loans, parking tickets, etc...) in the school's system preventing me from selecting classes, but I took it in stride. The former Kevin would've stressed out. If the jail system taught me anything, it was that there really isn't any other stress compared to being locked up.

It is a controlled environment; you are told when to eat, when to shower, and you realize what your family may be going through due to the choices you made. Having people with the controlling power telling you when to eat, sleep, use the phone, or having to be in the same room while someone else is taking a crap are all stress bombs. Inmates have no choice but to cope with it; unfortunately, some can't and just lose it. The latter should be enough for anyone to be scared straight.

Being back in school was like a dream come true; it was simply preordained. There was no doubt in my mind that I was going to be in those classrooms A.S.A.P. and it didn't matter if I had to walk ten miles to get there. Gorgeous females from all over the world were on the campus. I didn't care if they were fat, flat, slim, thick, blonde, brunette, weaved, brown, black, red, Asian, white, or ugly. I was as horny as an elephant in heat. Most females that I would spit my game to were just to sharpen my game, something I'd advise guys to do if they feel rusty. My intentions were to get with the ladies that had money or at least appeared to have access to it. The best way to do this was to hunt down the ladies in the parking lot because it meant they at least had a car. I collected a lot of numbers, but nothing really developed other than studying, smoking, and drinking partners.

Slowly I noticed that my focus on education was deteriorating because women were taking up much of my study time. Women are emotional beings that thrive on attention, and lots of it. They were costing me time and we all know the saying, "time is money." I was determined to get the best grades, but the females were in the way, so I dropped them completely for the time being. From then on, it was business only when I was on campus. The only females that I would date were ladies I met off campus. Besides the opposite sex, there were many other things about college life I missed, such as the power of being around the books in the library, conversing with my professors, and the all-you-can-eat buffets.

It felt good eating breakfast on campus again. At the price of about five dollars, anyone could eat like a king. Fresh, made-to-order eggs, huge waffles, five different cereals to choose from, chopped up fresh fruits of all sorts (pineapples were my favorites), five types of juices to choose from, two different milks, bacon, sausages, and five different breads. The ladies and fellas behind bars would lose their minds in a cafeteria like this. I would eat until my stomach was about to burst. I only ate like this twice a week or three times if I was balling.

Breathless is the only word to describe how it felt to be back in the classroom. I was given the opportunity to live my dream again. This time around I wasn't going to fumble any opportunities or drop any passes. This time I was playing to win in the game of life. Some of the bigger courses like my Astronomy or Geology courses (with 300 or more students) were held in auditoriums. I enjoyed them at first because they reminded me of the classes I saw in the movies, but in reality, they were difficult to learn in. It was too noisy and there were far too many distractions. Nonetheless, being in the presence of brilliant minds always appealed to me, no matter what environment I was in. Whether I was in the hood under a tree, on a city bus, or in a classroom, brain wrestling with and listening to intelligent people is something I take pleasure in…wisdom—priceless!

As I learned from the 1954 *Brown vs. the Board of Education* case, other than the usual racist perspectives, school was a place where poor and middle class students could mingle. Different cultures and backgrounds feed off each other mentally and God forbid, physically; this was what made college, college. Back in the day before official universities, there were places where philosophers would sit around in an area to share their thoughts and theories on any given subject. This is how the institution of the university was formed.

There were times I felt like I didn't belong around all these law-abiding students at the university I attended. For a brief period of time, the brainwashing of the jail system had me believing that I was permanently underclass; that's how the system wanted others in my shoes to feel and think, but I was determined not to be a statistic of recidivism. I was not going to move backwards from here on out. My mind was moving forward, no matter what. Lying on the financial aid application was how I received money from the government (there's a section that asks if you've ever been convicted of a crime and each and every semester I would answer "no"). I'm sure it was a crime and I could've written "yes" and took the risk of not getting the necessary funds to stay in school — or, I could continue lying and crossing my fingers in hopes of getting free money so that down the road, there would be a diploma waiting for me. I've taken many risks that could've resulted in me losing my freedom or my life. Taking a chance against the government or the beast itself in the name of education was

The Courage To Believe

worth it for me. I can respect someone lying and/or stealing to eat as long as they aren't physically hurting anyone else.

My ducks were all lined up and I was ready to play football again. I dealt with the same emotions that I felt in the classroom, the "I don't belong here" syndrome. I have to tip my hat to anyone who participates in sports at the collegiate level, especially football. The practices were the most physically challenging that my body has ever experienced. Even, my mental strength was pushed to the limit. We would line up two against two, about five yards apart and hit each other upon ordinances. None of us ever wanted to appear weak or hurt, so we would continue to hit each other viciously, helmet to helmet.

Football practices would take place at 6:00 a.m. before the sun would rise, so we would literally practice in the dark for about an hour. I was attempting to walk-on the team as a cornerback. My body was nothing but heart and muscle standing at 6'1", 180 pounds … thin in comparison to the other guys weighing at least 200 pounds. The coaches learned my last name in no time because no matter how many times I got knocked down, I'd pop back up ready to go right back at it. Sometimes I was the one knocking them down. There was no shortage of defensive backs causing the competition to be steep, but I wasn't scared. What did I have to lose? Just a month ago I was in lockup singing the "Jail House Rock." I was enjoying every bit of my freedom, education, and the practices.

Nonetheless, making the football team was not the most important thing to me, the education was. Making the team wasn't going to be as much of a problem as getting a starting position. Nevertheless, I gave it all I had for one spring season expecting to receive some sort of financial assistance, but to no avail, so I walked away.

The choices we make in life will either make you or break you. This may sound crazy, but going to jail was the best thing that could have happened to me. It's like suddenly sitting straight up in bed after a very bad dream, but realizing "thankfully" it was only a dream. My appetite for breaking the law and chancing going back to jail was no longer an option on the menu. It was replaced with purpose and destiny. I was now, more than ever, focused and determined to avoid that path by any means necessary. Once you're locked up and you are surrounded by concrete walls and bars, you sadly realize that you have nothing but time…. no pun intended, and your choices robbed you of your freedom. The freedom to wake up, go to sleep, eat, drink, watch T.V., sing out loud, take a bath or shower for hours and then walk around your room naked or whatever you desire, you no longer have the freedom to make any of those choices. As a matter of fact, your choices are very limited and are made for you with very strict conditions. If you find yourself behind bars, it is critical, that you begin to feed your mind and spirit with uplifting books, preferably the Word of God and also physical exercise for your body. Many of us become institutionalized in our minds and actually feel more comfortable caged away. And if that happens, chances are, you will become repeat offenders making the same choices or worse, landing you right back where you don't want to be. Everything that was once important to you i.e., your family, friends, relationships, and life itself are placed on hold.

The Courage To Believe

Little did I know that it was impossible to stay out of jail being on "papers." Being on "papers" is nothing but being in jail while out of jail. Even so, the latter of the two seemed to be more appealing. I was sentenced to five years and eight months "papers." The eight months were knocked out of the way with the bid I did. Ain't that something? I was on probation while behind bars, which was cool with me. The length of my probation was trimmed in half. Most people can never successfully finish their probation, since one is under close scrutiny. The system is built to allow you back into society completely freed once you've been convicted and served your time, regardless of the crime. Once you have a case number, consider it as a new social security number. You're left walking on eggshells. In fact, that's how I succeeded; by walking a straight path simply by running away from the scent of trouble and troublemakers.

"There are *only* three places you should be," Judge Elijah Williams advised me, "Church, school, or work."

According to him, this was the only way to get off "papers" early, if at all. However, things were about to get interesting sooner than expected once I was back home.

A week of freedom and I was already arrested. Wow! On a weekday morning, my mom woke me up before she went to work and told me not to go outside because she had a dream that one of us (her sons) got arrested. She has told me similar stories, countless of times, but this time it was different due to the fact she never woke me up to tell me of a nightmare.

By nightfall, my brother Pharo and I decided to watch a film called "The Hurricane," based on a true story starring Denzel Washington as the main actor. This movie happens to be about an African American boxer, Rubin "Hurricane" Carter, a former American middleweight boxer who competed from 1961 through 1966. Carter, along with John Artis, was convicted twice for the 1966 bar murder of three white people in his hometown. He was later released after serving twenty years of three life sentences when a federal judge overturned his conviction. So Pharo and I were getting rowdy because of the injustice that Carter and Artis had to go through when we heard a loud knock on the door, which always makes my heart jump out of my chest because only the police would disrespect a person's house like that. We peaked through the windows and sure enough, there's a swarm of police officers surrounding the house. We had everything from guns to weed in the house ... more than enough to violate my freedom papers with multiple new charges, and without a doubt, decapitating my dreams of finishing school. *My personal Waterloo*! We didn't panic because we both had street smarts and time to come up with a plan.

The officer who was pounding on the door was a sergeant. We didn't answer, but they knew at least one person was inside. I told my brother not to open the door, but ask them if they had a warrant.

"We don't have a warrant, we just want to ask a couple of questions," the sergeant replies.

"No warrant, no entry," I told Pharo to tell them.

The Courage To Believe

This back and forth chatter lasted for about two hours. All those officers to ask a few questions ... hmmm, that didn't make any sense; but what really threw me off was the fact they didn't have a warrant, which was great news for us. No warrant, then why so many cops? They were walking all around the house, stepping on our mom's flowers, banging on the front and back doors, embarrassing our home in front of neighbors, and flashing their flash lights through the windows. It was as if there were slave catchers coming to catch the runaways, which was exactly how it felt. After a while, arresting us didn't seem like such a bad idea because our mom was going to go berserk once she sees her flowers mangled (she loved gardening vegetables and bright flowers).

The bottom-line was, no matter what, we couldn't allow them to come into the house. My brother was toying with them, tapping on the windows since we knew they couldn't kick in the door without a warrant. However, my mother was coming from work real soon, so I knew we had to leave because she would've let them in. Prison time for me would've been definite once they got inside and searched. I would've taken all of the charges, and honestly Pharo would've done the same- two warrior kings. By this time, I could see my college dreams and hopes of getting back on top of the world going down the drain and I was adjusting to being back in school. Contending for your life should come naturally, especially when life is a blessing with all its abundant treasures.

Next, we devised a plan to get arrested outside of the house. I really wanted to have Pharo go with them and shut the door behind him. They were going to get him regardless, being a suspect that they would bring all that manpower (about fifteen police officers) to capture. However, I couldn't let my brother go out by himself. I'll do anything for my family.

Fortunately for us, they left just in time. We waited a few minutes and drove to the nearest train station that was only three miles away. An unmarked car followed us, but for some reason, a random car stopped in front of us and forced me to mash on the breaks causing my car to hit a 360 turn in the middle of downhill traffic. Miraculously, we weren't hit by another car! We stopped, smiled at each other, took a deep breath, and hit it to the station. As soon as I dropped Pharo off, a K-9 unit raced in as I exited the station; I had seen him in the rearview hitting a U-turn. I was able to swallow the three rocks that we had in the car before they arrested the both of us.

They charged Pharo with assault with a firearm, which didn't make sense since they came to the house for "questioning." They charged me with aiding an escape. The truth of the matter was they arrested me for being on probation.

How was it possible for me to aid the escape of someone that didn't have a warrant for his arrest or wasn't locked up?

Guilty or not guilty, any arrest would guarantee another warrant since I was on "papers." And what do you know ... another week out of school spent wasted in jail. The charges were dropped against me after all because legally neither of us should've been arrested. I didn't want to go to court that day, but Ms. Byrd, my counselor at FAU, and my mom were constantly on my case about it. Glad they were, for love shows who truly care for you in the storms of life.

Ms. Byrd always impressed me with her immaculate dress code, her mahogany and gold office, and her cranberry-colored Mercedes. This African American woman had class and power; the very essence of my dream woman. I was honored when she asked me to do a video interview with a police captain on crime prevention. I prepared for the interview by tying up my neatly washed, shoulder length dreads, a Burberry shirt with khaki pants, and cocaine white Reeboks.

I knew I was innocent, but the officers were quick to arrest me due to the fact that jail business is big business. The local, state, and federal government makes a lot of money when individuals are incarcerated. The going rate for each person incarcerated is about $100.00 a day from the government. Every day that someone is in jail, the county bills the state about $100.00 to babysit the inmates (Assembly Committee On Public Safety). From my experience it seems as if seventy percent of the people in the Broward county jail are there for probation violations. I guess that's how these public officials continually allocate six figure salaries. Helping them to get rich at the price of my freedom wasn't part of my purpose or destiny.

I vowed then, never to go back to jail with God's help. Once again, I realized that was impossible while on probation and being black male, because everyday was like walking on thin ice. We may choose our paths, but the Lord directs our steps and I walked carefully. At this point of my life, I wasn't walking with Christ completely or consistently attending church, so hearing the voice of God through the Holy Spirit wasn't the same as it would have been for a more seasoned and obedient servant.

People think that if you are on probation and do everything you're supposed to, that violating probation won't happen. That's just not true. Your freedom isn't yours anymore. It's at the state's discretion (the police, the probation officers, or the judge). Due to the choices I made, this evil door was opened in my life, but I was standing on the Word of God along with His grace and mercy that He was going to close it. Most of the POs (probation officers) were mean, but I must admit, two of them were cool and both happened to be women (one was black and the other was a very attractive white woman that took a liking to my ambition). I remember this particular PO, a heavy-set white woman who enjoyed her power over me a little too much. She actually yelled at me over the phone for not changing my address on my driver license. I quickly filed a complaint to switch my PO before she violated me on some foolishness.

I was told three things by an ol' coon (old inmate) before my release: first, do not play games with my PO's, second, don't get too comfortable on the streets, and third, switch POs if there's a negative vibe because they'll violate you. I was learning to listen to wisdom very well.

For everyone that is on parole or "papers," I would like to share from experience, a few easy tips you can follow to successfully receive your "freedom papers." In my mind, it was either have guaranteed jail time, or have the freedom to enjoy your family, good food, making money, and courting a lovely woman. What a tough choice .... right?

<u>TIP ONE:</u> Smoking weed is a sure way to violate parole. Stop smoking, it's not worth it! That five-dollar can cost you your freedom and a hundred times more money in the end.

<u>TIP TWO:</u> If you're in school, don't let them know you've got a job simply because school is more than enough to get them off of your back. Education is music to the judges' ears so use it to your advantage. If the PO knows where you work, then they will call to verify your employment if they want to be nasty, even though they really don't have to, depending on the level of your case (remember, this only applies if you are in school).

<u>TIP THREE:</u> Some employers don't do background checks; they know that nobody else but felons would be crazy enough, or perhaps, desperate enough to take the job. Working in restaurants, telemarketing, or even starting your own business are awesome ideas. Please take my advice because they have worked marvelously for me.

<u>TIP FOUR:</u> This last, but not least point, I can't stress enough. Don't give the PO your cell number or house number if you can avoid it. They don't have to have a direct number to you as long as there is a number that they can leave a message; however, you'll need an address for them to visit to verify you live there. Giving them your cell phone number only gives them more access to harass you at will. These days they might even text you. For example, let's say your PO wants you to

come in, he or she can give you a time limit, and if you don't come in on time, guess what happens? You get an automatic V.O.P. (Violation of Probation), even if you reported a couple of days prior. They do this to give those they supervise a surprise drug test. In my case, I wasn't doing drugs, but had a life. Reporting once a month was too much, not to mention I had productive things to do with my time. Three years on "papers" and the system never had a direct number by which to contact me. All they needed to know was that I couldn't afford a phone because I was a "struggling student," but I actually did have a phone; I made use of the payphones whenever the need to reach them came up.

My probation was based in Palm Beach County because that's where I was living, however, my case originated in Broward County, which is south of Palm Beach County and north of Miami-Dade County. I was ordered to pay $150.00 a month for restitution fees in correlation to my charges. My PO was breathing down my back like a dragon about the payments as if she was a bill collector for the I.R.S. So I asked her if it was possible for me to see a judge to reduce my payments. She said, "No," and if I did, it would be a violation because I would have to leave the county, which is against the terms of my probation.

Regardless, my intentions were to go against her will without permission or a lawyer. The night before heading down to Broward County Court house, I was able to catch a train to Fort Lauderdale in time to find a P.D. officer or "Public Defender" as she was leaving her office. She gave me step-by-step instructions on what to do the next morning while we were

The Courage To Believe

walking to the elevators. She told me to be extremely polite and to dress professionally before speaking to the deputy in the courtroom who would theoretically announce me to the judge. "You can't just go directly to him and disrupt court while it's in session. You don't want to end up on your neck," she told me.

Judge Elijah Williams, a black male and the only black judge at that time in the Broward County courthouse, was pretty fair-minded. Keep in mind there were no court dates. So, I closed my eyes and prayed.

"Your Honor, I'm Kevin Dorival and would like to ask you and the court to listen to my request, for reduction of my P.O. fees, I am a college student and can't afford this, sir."

Judge Elijah said, "Well Good Morning, sir."

"Who's your lawyer and which school do you attend?" the judge asked.

"Florida Atlantic University your Honor and God is my Council," I replied with a bold spirit ... suddenly, the nervousness went away.

The judge shouted, "Amen! I haven't seen you in my courtroom in a while. That's a great thing. Alright, Mr. Dorival, I'll be glad to listen to your request. Have a seat. I'll be ready to have lunch with my staff after hearing what you have to say.... Lunch is on you, correct?"

We all laughed in the courtroom. He was in a good mood so timing was perfect.

He reduced my supervision payments to zero dollars. I only had to pay the restitution, which was $35.00 a month or whatever I could pay as long as I was paying something until my restitution was paid up, on the grounds that I was in college with no job. This was a great victory and I didn't have to pay a lawyer to do it.

Judge Williams helped me out by canceling the cost of my supervision completely. He was a reasonable man and was obviously interested in helping people that were trying to help themselves, especially young black males. I also asked if he would make a note on record that I wasn't in violation for coming in to see him. It took a lot of guts to step up for myself like that, and I saved $500 by not paying a lawyer to make the request. My P.O. was not too pleased, but I won that battle hands down; yet the war wasn't over.

Shortly thereafter, I was employed at the Student Government (S.G.) office of Florida Atlantic University. The person that got me the gig was the Study Student Body President, Ancel Mratt, another black male. I lied about my felony record to get this job so I could have a little money in my pocket, especially with gas prices doubling to two dollars, a huge difference from my high school days. Students today in 2012 are paying close to $3.75 (or more) per gallon for gas. I'm almost embarrassed to say it sometimes, but I was basically the S.G. secretary for the University-Wide Council (UWC) meetings that took place twice a month. My job duties were to record the meetings with a tiny digital Olympus recorder and write down on paper what was important enough to take note of. Women are usually secretaries but I was willing to suck it up in the name of *money*. The hardest part of my job was typing the main points of the meetings, which usually lasted two to three hours, sometimes more. We ate very well after every meeting, especially if the meeting was out of town.

The meetings taught me a lot about delegating, politics, and arguing in a polite fashion. For example, if a student organization needed funds for a project of up to $5,000 dollars, a vote of 12 was required; two representatives from each of the six F.A.U. campuses across South Florida that made up the quorum. After about two months in S.G., I found another job at Red Lobster, so I was working two part-time jobs at the same time and going to school. Working hard was never a problem for me. As a result, I worked in the S.G. organization for two years.

SIXTEEN

LIFE IN EXILE

Every year of my life seemed to go by the flip of a coin. One year would be very good and seemingly on cloud nine and the next ... a living nightmare. I didn't understand in my adolescent years that the choices I made then would significantly affect my future. It's almost as if the devil jumped in and Jesus jumped out. The fact is, Jesus was always there, I just wasn't looking for Him. Perhaps it was that I didn't practice the importance of planting good seeds, which would enable me to reap a good harvest. I'm willing to bet that this is what our youth are suffering from today; investing in bad habits and behaviors that will cause a harvest of destruction and turmoil in their lives.

Life in 2003 was pretty good. The stability of attending school had returned and I began a steady relationship with a young lady that turned out to be the love of my life, Arianna "Baby Cakes" Michellete. I also had a nice "horse" (my car), an '85 Cutlass Supreme painted Benz Blue to match the blue in the large Haitian flag laid across my dash board. Where I'm from, dressing up older cars was a big hit throughout the Dirty South, especially in Florida. The paint on my horse was so wet that I got tickets for breaking the water restrictions. That year was certainly rated as an "off the chain" year.

The Courage To Believe

Not so with 2004 – it was the exact opposite of the previous year! Little did I know, things were about to get a tad bit crazy! By mid-2003, I moved out of my mother's home because of the disagreements I was having with her husband. I even believed that he may have poisoned me with my mother's food. I informed her of my concerns, but she didn't believe me. At times, the tension in the atmosphere was so thick in the house that you could with a knife. On several occasions, the police had to be called because of our arguments. Let me also remind you that I don't like cops and I was still on "papers" (probation), but thank God no arrests were ever made when they came. Things really got heated on our return trip back home from my sister's graduation in Orlando.

My sister Kerlene was about to graduate from Bryman (now Everest College) in Orlando so mom, Kerlene, Donald (her boyfriend), Greg (a cousin), and I planned a trip to the "O" (Orlando) for the graduation ceremony. We were going in two separate cars; my cousin Greg and I in one and the rest of them in another. They ended up leaving 15 minutes before us because Kerlene became irritated with me for wanting to eat something before hitting the road for the two and a half hour trip. She was worried about getting caught up in Friday's traffic. It's my philosophy to never leave home without eating, especially on a long trip (also never without wearing clean and hole-less underwear) ... that's how we were raised. One never knows whether it could be their last meal. Besides, why take a trip out of town without eating something? Minutes before the argument, Donald and I had a brief conversation about the trip and he mentioned the name of my sister's school.

Nonetheless, they left without us and we were on our own to drive to Orlando. The funny thing is, I had never driven to the "O" on my own before. I could've simply stayed home, but I wouldn't have been able to live with myself if I had missed her graduation. It was a big day for our family and I had to be there to support her. We ate breakfast, stopped to get some weed and liquor and off we went on our road trip adventure. We only knew the time of the graduation, but not the location where the ceremony was to take place.

When we arrived in Orlando, it was raining cats and dogs. To make matters worse, we didn't know exactly where to go from there. We got off at an exit to find a hotel to use their payphone because service through cell phone carrier was local and wouldn't work in Orlando back then. We called our cousins Mo and West that lived in the city to come to our rescue. While they were on their way to the hotel, I was flirting with the clerk at the front desk. I explained to her our situation, and she immediately knew the school's name by the part of the name I could remember...High Tech Institute. She knew the school as Bryman College/High Tech Institute (now called Everest). She looked it up in the yellow pages and called up the school. Whoever she was speaking to gave her the place and time of the graduation. Greg and I surprised the heck out of my mom and sister when we arrived at the graduation. It was as if they saw a ghost.

We all hit the road immediately after the graduation. As soon as we got to Mom's house that night, my mom's husband and I got into a heated argument over the back garage door. He didn't like for me to use that door because his lawn equipment was in the garage, so, he boarded it up to prevent thieves from gaining access. My mom knew I used that back door frequently for years. I took the boards off and it angered her, and out of frustration and I'm sure at the persistence of her husband, she called the police while I was in the shower.

I was shocked that officers called me out of the bathroom and told me to come outside the house. I didn't do anything or offend my mother at all. Her husband got into her head to be against me. He was the breadwinner, but my money was talking just as loud as his. She was caught in between our macho standoff, but I was too grown to be under his control.

My heart was beating really hard and fast, even though I knew I didn't break any laws. Being in and out of the system since an adolescent, I naturally developed paranoia of cops. Once outside, they ran my name through their system to check for warrants. One of the four officers was trying to provoke me to do something negative, and we got into an argument.

Once the cops left, I went off on my mom. I was very upset with her for siding with her deceitful husband to call the police on me, knowing how I felt about them. And before I knew what I was saying, I called her the "B" word. My mom kicked me out! I knew then, that if I could call *her* that, I could call *any* woman *anything*. I have the highest respect for my mother; this was the first and only time I ever disrespected her. I really felt badly after doing it, and it bothers me 'til this day. Whatever possessed me to do such a thing? The decision to move had already been made, so I called my sisters and told them I needed a place to stay. They welcomed me since they had always wanted me to move in with them ever since my father moved out, leaving the house man-less.

The next morning, I moved to Pembroke Pines. My sisters Suzanne, Yandie, Judie, and I have the same father. They lived so far out west it was ridiculous! The only reason someone would move that far out was to hide from someone. Nevertheless, for the first time, I was in a peaceful neighborhood in a gated community. Across the street from their house was an FBI agent. Three houses down from us was a lovely black couple with two kids. That couple's home was beautiful and they had two matching, grey Mercedes Benzes. They appeared to live the life I one day aspire to have: a faithful and beautiful wife, beautiful kids, a dog, and the finances to travel whenever we desire.

My sister's place was very nice also. I was always impressed by their home's interior decorating. My room was the master bedroom, which had a fancy bathroom; it consisted of a standing shower and tub/Jacuzzi; how can I forget the walk- in, double - door closet? I didn't have nearly as many clothes and shoes for a closet that size, but I did coordinate my miniature wardrobe by color from brightest to darkest. Someday, I would love to live in West Pembroke Pines again, but I must have a helicopter to be able to fly back and forth.

Living in that house was like that MTV reality show "The Real World." It was bananas most of the times! There were three girls – all teenagers, with no adults. The oldest was twenty-two and there were no parents living with them. Their mother died in a horrible car accident in 1995, and my father, the player, only checked up on them once in a while or whenever he needed money. The city of Miami was paying them yearly for the loss of their mom since it was the police's fault for chasing a speeding suspect through traffic. All three of them had a boyfriend of some sort. Girls will be girls, and they lived the way they wanted to. I love my sisters, but they lacked discipline and respect for themselves, not to mention their home. I even witnessed Judie, the youngest at the age of 14, get drunk and vomit all over the place.

This was my junior year at FAU and I had to drive one and a half hours, five days a week to get to school. I was still holding down my two part-time-gigs at the time while going to a church called Mount Olive in Miami on Wednesday nights and Sunday mornings. Robert McCullough, a friend who I met visiting another church convinced me to draw closer to God by staying in His Word and continue going to church.

"The more time you spend with God, the less time the devil has to bother you," he would often say.

This quote remained embedded in my heart forever. Humbling myself to listen to my spirit began at this stage—my own personal "Great Awakening." I was getting pruned for a war with no idea the battle had already begun when I cursed at my mother. Out of all the crazy things I've done in my life, that brief moment in time had to be the most extreme up-to-that point; I disrespected a woman and even worse, my own mom. That night, I set my world on fire with my tongue according to James 3:6 NIV:

"And the tongue is a flame of fire; it is a whole of wickedness, corrupting your entire body. It can set your whole life on fire, for it is set on fire by hell itself."

Words are very powerful and I was just about to experience the evil side of them.

My sisters had a cousin who was part of a rap group that would often use their living room as a studio. Groups of people would be in recording sessions at all times of the night… and into the early morning. I was working long hours at Red Lobster after school and sometimes in Student Government. I often was too tired to hear anything, so I basically slept through the racket and held my tongue. It was inevitable that one day I would get tired of the ruckus and escort them out, Lord help me! In order to make it to class (Poetry Course) on time, I would have to be up by 6:30 AM and on the interstate by 7:00 AM, before sunrise. These Negroes were up eating us out of house and home and making noise as if no one was sleeping. They would smoke cigarettes and weed in the house; I smoked weed too, but never in the house. My sisters acted like they were scared to say something, so as politely as possible, I told them to leave. I was on bad terms at the time with Yandie, the second oldest, so she encouraged them to continue with their noise campaign to get back at me.

The Courage To Believe

Their house was a cesspool of drama. I eventually found refuge in jogging and swimming at the clubhouse within the community gates. There was also a Jacuzzi and I spent many hours unwinding there. I knew that eventually, I would have to move out of the house because the drama was escalating like the price of gas.

After three months, out of nowhere, suddenly my oldest sister Suzanne hated me. One night, she wanted to pick her up from the hospital, but I didn't want to because she had friends that were already coming to get her. But for whatever reason, she wanted me to do it. I could only think it was because she didn't want me to use the house phone to talk with my girl. When her friends brought her home, she kicked opened my door and threw a television remote control at my head which landed on my right eyebrow causing a trickle of blood to run down my face. Suzanne was pregnant at the time with her first child, so I didn't retaliate or even say a word, but instead moved out immediately that night with some of my clothes.

My money was funny at the time, so I couldn't get my own place. My focus was to continue school no matter what I was going through, where I lived, or how I lived; it just didn't matter. At least, that's how I conditioned myself to think because there were plenty of times that I wanted to give up. In my head, I was reminded that it was better than being in jail. One thing for sure is that I needed a place to stay… ASAP!

I asked my auntie, Greg's mom, if I could temporarily move in with them since she was my closest auntie and she said, "No," due to issues with the landlord. I spent so many nights sleeping over on the weekends that I thought it wouldn't be a problem to stay there. In fact, I asked a few of my relatives, but to no avail.

Meanwhile, my mother wanted me to move back in with her now that her marriage wasn't working out. As stubborn as the Pharaoh was in the book of Genesis, I wouldn't move back. Soon after, I moved in with my Uncle Joe. He had a small, roach infested apartment, but he welcomed me with open arms. He was always our favorite uncle because he exposed us to the world ... fun things many parents would do if they had extra money. He took us to see our first movie, which was about Native Americans hunting in the snow. I saw my first gun and how to cook cocaine from him when I was probably about seven. The only thing I didn't like about him was that he would beat the dog crap out of his girlfriends. I witnessed him beat his women and saw the alterations he did to their faces. I don't know why any of them ever stayed with him after the first whooping. He would beat them regularly like they were sparing partners for a local fight.

Nonetheless, living with him was cool at first, but he was always in my pocket— thirty dollars here, one hundred dollars there. It came to a point that I had to lie about not having money in order to have money just to purchase my schoolbooks. Now, I would give my last dollar to my loved ones, but not to anyone that wouldn't do the same for me. Watching him get mad at his girlfriend, I knew it was a matter of time before he would beat her or attempt to fight me. His behavior was unpredictable and I wasn't about to stick around for the grand finale.

Living with Uncle Joe wasn't the best experience due to his issues; they brought him a great deal of stress. Money issues were making him crazier and meaner by the day—a monster. I was rarely at their apartment due to being a full-time student with two part-time jobs. I didn't mind the cold morning showers or getting my car scratched up by the over packed parking lot, but the truth of the matter is, I was avoiding him at all costs. Whenever my uncle would catch me at the apartment, he'd start complaining about his money needs! On top of that, my auntie, who was an illegal citizen that couldn't find meaningful work after a serious surgery to her liver, needed money. Uncle Joe was also having IRS problems for claiming other people's kids on his taxes (people in the ghetto are infamous for this around tax season). Moreover, he believed that if the microwave timer wasn't on zero, it was burning electricity and was adamant about that. What put the nail in the coffin was when I realized that ironing my clothes pissed him off because he felt it made the electricity bill higher. While ironing my clothes for church on a Sunday morning, this is what my uncle said to me,

"You can't iron your clothes every day," he commented.

In my head, I was like, "Bro, are you for real?" In life, you really find out who your true family and friends are when times get rough. When they have the choice of helping you with their last plate of food or last dollar, they would rather turn their backs on you and allow you to be devoured by the wolves. However, we all have our imperfections. I guess you really *don't* know anyone until you live with them; those welcoming smiles seemed to fade away. This great uncle of mine was losing points fast, but I still loved him. However, the decision to leave was an easy one.

Uncle Joe and I had a close relationship, but that relationship vanished when his true colors blossomed at a time when I needed him the most. *"One hand washes the other"* is a code I live by.

Baby Cakes was the best friend to me that everyone wished they could have. She was the only one I could talk to outside of my family and was very supportive. I remember once speaking to her about the conditions at my uncle's apartment and I almost broke down crying. Baby Cakes and I met November of 2003 at an FAU football game in Ft. Lauderdale. She was with her best friend Cloretta and I was with my little sister Judie. When I first saw Baby Cakes and Cloretta, it was a tough choice on my part on which one to approach. Baby Cakes was beautiful, sexy, and slim while her friend was voluptuous, but not nearly as cute. So what I decided to do was to approach them at the same time and wait to see which one gave me a sign of interest. Voilà! Baby Cakes was wagging her tail as I introduced myself to the both of them. She had a charisma about her that could cheer up a funeral…very unique.

The Courage To Believe

Our relationship was peaches and cream for the first couple of months. She made me wait two months before we got involved intimately, and I respected her for it. We clicked so well and she caught me at a good time in my life, but the coin was getting ready to flip; however, before it flipped, she saw how romantic I could be. One night, I filled up the Jacuzzi with hot water and bubbles and surrounded it with candles. Baby Cakes was the last female for a very long time to get that treatment and she was fortunate to experience the Casanova in me.

All the fun was short lived as a result of the drama on my part. Drama brings stress and stress needs sex—lots of it. I quickly moved out just as fast as I moved into my uncle's spot. After apologizing to my mother for my outbursts, I was welcomed to move back in. By this time, it was early February and my birthday was around the corner. Baby Cakes and I were growing fonder of each other. Her sense of humor was impeccable and so was the way she supported me. The love word started flowing in the air, and, I met her mother so it was time for her to meet mine. The day she was supposed to meet my mom, she was called into work, so they settled for a phone conversation.

Later that same week on Saturday, it was my 25th birthday. When Friday came around I was excited and filled with so much anticipation. I left my International Political Issues course earlier and went home to wash my car. I also wanted to snatch my work clothes so when I left school I could head south to Miami and hang out with my cousins before I clocked in for work. Before I reached the car wash, a motorcycle cop pulled me over citing that my tints were too dark, but he let me slide since it was the eve of my birthday weekend. I washed my car while guzzling an "O.E." Old English malt liquor bottle and went home.

And the drama of '04 continued. On the way home, I bumped into a mechanic from the neighborhood who worked on my car, so I stopped my car to ask, "What's up!" I got out of the car and one of his friend's that had an issue with me in the past came out of nowhere and rushed me. No time to ask questions, I weaved out of the way and threw the OE bottle I was drinking at him. Strike! Quickly my punches were connecting left, right, left, and right, to his face. He was hitting me with some mediocre punches in the back and on the side of my shoulder. In the heat of the battle, I didn't realize that his punches weren't punches at all. Another guy who was with him, and whom I had never seen before, threw a brick at me, but missed. As I picked up the brick, I saw blood flowing down my right arm onto the grey brick. Then it hit me that the blood was coming from me and the soft punches were really stabs; all of a sudden, I felt sharp pains all over my back.

At this point, I was extremely weak and barely made it to my car that was still running in neutral. My house was around the corner, but it was a difficult drive due to the lack of strength in my arms, not to mention the blood that I was losing at a rapid pace. There were two of them, so I decided to leave while I was still breathing. To add insult to injury, as I left, one of them

The Courage To Believe

threw a brick through my back window. Boom! I didn't even look back to see the damage.

I made it home. I tried to call the ambulance, but my cell phone was acting up so I couldn't get through to an operator. I wanted to wait outside for someone to see me, but the flaming hot sun was draining my strength; it had to be at least ninety-four degrees. As I walked into the house, I disturbed my mom who was sleeping soundly, but was awaken by my sounds of agony. She called out my name, but I couldn't respond with words. Instinctively, mom sensed something was wrong. "Kevin, Kevin?" She saw and followed a massive trail of blood on her beautiful white tile floor from the front door to the bathroom. I could hear her screaming at the top of her lungs. She found me lying down in the tub fully clothed with the shower running. I could have used her bathroom since it was closer to the front door, but I didn't want to ruin her immaculately decorated bathroom.

She screamed in Creole, "Kevin, kisa yo fè pou ou, kisa yo fè pou ou?" That translates to, "Kevin, what have they done to you, what have they done to you?"

She ran out of the house and called the ambulance from her cell phone. I choose to lie in the tub because it was the only place I could think of that would contain the massive amount of blood.

An elderly woman appeared in the bathroom like an angel and asked:

"Is there anything I can get for you?"

"Some cold water please," I told her.

The water was so soothing to my parched throat. After gaining my senses I made two calls. First, I called my little brother Pharo, and left him a brief message about what just happened. Then I called Baby Cakes at her job and told her that I was sorry because I always seemed to mess up. She planned this big birthday for me at a fancy restaurant and hotel. Last thing I remember about the conversation was that she cried and the phone slipped out of my wet hands. Obviously, I wasn't thinking, using the phone while lying in the tub with the shower running. I'm not sure whether I was delusional or not, but the ambulance came pretty quick.

"He's blacking out," one of them said.

The ambulance woke me up as they carried me out of the house. I thought I was dreaming and wanted to wake up from this nightmare as soon as possible. The realization of what was happening to me was surreal. The possibility of a nightmare vanished once I was on the stretcher under the scorching sun; the sunrays were like kryptonite to Superman on my skin. The pain was excruciating beyond the value of any words. This was the worst pain I had ever felt in my life. My whole body felt like it had stab wounds. Couldn't believe this was really happening to me.

The Courage To Believe

In the emergency room, the nurses cut off my favorite jeans from the leg up to the belt. There wasn't any wound below my chest, but they wanted to make sure. These were a nice pair of jeans, but at the time, I didn't care about anything, but surviving. "Do what you have to do to get me out of this place," was mainly my thought. They did a bunch of procedures before my mom and sister was allowed in the emergency room. The look on their faces spoke a thousand words. Baby Cakes left her job and came in with a smile on her face, desperately trying to change the mood in the room. Pharo and Gar, a friend of mine, came in shortly after. These individuals are basically my allies for life; they are the ones that were there for me then and are the same ones here for me now. During the entire time I was in the ER, a patient screamed for morphine to numb his pain. He jumped off a moving motorcycle attempting a stunt that broke all his ribs, his nose, and I forgot the rest. He was really messed up!

The angel of death missed me that afternoon. It wasn't my time. In total, there were 13 stab wounds, and two of them were so deep that it looked like a tunnel. Surprisingly, the thought of dying never crossed my mind. My thoughts were how I was going to get back to class. I was missing a test that took me two weeks to study for. That's when it hit me that I was dead serious about my education – my future. If I was given an option, I would've gone straight to class to take my test that same day. The hospital kept me there overnight for some testing. I told them that I didn't have insurance and it was then I learned that the state pays the medical bills of victims. I just wanted to at least be home for my 25th birthday, so I snuck out the hospital the next day, February 7, 2005.

Meanwhile, I cooperated with the police the best I could by answering their questions. Dank, the culprit, had to be brought to justice, one-way or the other. For the first time in my life, I felt like a victim. My days would have been cut short if I wasn't able to fight back. I'm convinced that he would have stabbed me to death. I was really pissed off and wanted the police to catch him, but they couldn't find a face with the name I gave them. The detectives only worked at the station two days a week. The station was so cheap; they had detectives that seemed to work as independent contractors on cases when their schedules permitted. I could feel my blood bubbling with emotion at their inactivity with the case. All I could see were Dank's gold teeth shining…taunting me.

I was too weak to take my own baths for a couple of weeks, but the following Tuesday, I went back to school against my mom's and doctor's advice.

I believe that in everyone's life comes a moment that presents itself on a platinum platter.

You only have one chance to make the right decision; laying down waiting for my wounds to heal would have been a foolish decision. Going back to school was simply the will in me and I was not letting anyone or anything stop me from the mission of graduating – plain and simple; never spoke of losing or giving up even though I wanted to sometimes. My family's encouragement reaffirmed my dreams and aspirations at a time when my spirit was down. Their very presence made my heart smile. Victory was going to be mine if I could hold tight to my faith. My mom prayed and read the Bible with me, which was something we hadn't done together since high school. The mood would change once I told her that one day I was going to buy her a Jaguar to replace her car had once crashed back in high school. She always smiled when I told her that. "Thank you my son," she would say with a warm smile.

Looking back at the situation, it was so much easier said than done to remain in school. From elementary to college, school was the only place I felt safe and stable. I must admit that the stabbing left me shell shocked, but I was comfortable enough to forget about it while I was in class and focused on the remaining weeks of that spring semester.

Being able to smell my own flesh for weeks infuriated me all the more. That's just how deep the wounds were. Many nights I would have nightmares about getting shot or stabbed to death. The devil was tormenting me under the sun and the moon. Every weekday I would be excited to sit in a classroom because the courses overshadowed what was really going on in my crazy world. It made me wonder how many other students were going through hard times and still able to focus. That question would be answered years later.

My stats (statistics) class was my hardest course, so I withdrew in order to invest more time in my other courses. It was ironic that my Law and American Society course spoke about black on black crime statistics right after the horrible stabbing incident. The General Psychology course that had about four hundred students was my favorite course. Classes were held in a huge, brand new auditorium. Learning about myself appealed to me the most, other than learning about the minds of geniuses and theologians, both of whom have intriguing thoughts. Sigmund Freud was also an interesting character with all of his theories. The professor, Dr. Natons, who is a very bright woman, made a statement in a sarcastic tone.

"I am a Psychology Professor not a psychologist, so please don't come to my office with your life issues expecting treatment," she warned.

Everybody busted out laughing; I think I laughed the hardest among the students. Surprisingly, I finished that course with an "A," but it was not easy.

Two months had passed since my birthday and my body healed up pretty good on the exterior. The doctor said it would take a year until my body's interior would be healed fully enough to be able to continue my regular routines. I was ready to go back to work and I did so about 10 months earlier than the doctors recommended. My co-workers showed me a lot of love when I came back. All the attention got my spirits back up since I was real down about life around that time. Everyone stopped working to give me a standing ovation and hugs.

Almost a year later, I was back in the swing of things and all the negativity was put behind me until my sister, Kerlene, got a visit from three homicide detectives. They wanted to speak to me about a recent shooting that took place. I was in class when Kerlene texted me about their visit. I had moved months ago without the knowledge of my parole officer, Mr. Schineheadburger ("Mr. S." The only reason I remembered his name is because it's so strange). I never transferred to the closest probation office because Mr. S. never wasted my time when I would visit. Most POs would make me or anyone else wait thirty minutes to a couple of hours before being seen for their monthly report which only took literally 1-3 minutes. I personally think some of the POs enjoyed the power of making us wait, knowing that we couldn't leave, especially if that was the only day we could report. He would have me wait no longer than 10 minutes. Therefore, I left Palm Beach County and moved back to Broward County, but kept Mr. S., which was an obvious violation, but he never checked up on me anyway. The state loves to keep track of their money, and ex-cons like me were considered assets. I was worth more to the system locked up than I was free.

The detectives wanted me to come in for some questioning and left a business card for me. The next day, I received a call from a friend telling me Dank was killed the day before. My friend, whose name will remain anonymous, was enthusiastic about telling me because he knew how much the whole situation affected us, my family, and friends. Instantly mixed emotions hit me all at once. There was a joy inside me to know that he wasn't a threat any longer, but at the same time, I was mad knowing I didn't get to settle the score myself. In anticipation of unwanted attention, I visited my lawyer and also reminded my mom to make sure she told my PO or anyone else that was looking for me that I still resided there.

As soon as he told me this unraveling news, I knew that I would be a prime suspect because of our prior altercation and my arrest record. I also knew I wouldn't be the only suspect. Dank, may he rest in peace, was a neighborhood troublemaker. His face was dirty on the streets. He supposedly stabbed a couple of guys at several nightclubs. Someone like him had to hide under rocks and constantly switch cars for cover since he had unfinished business with so many other enemies. The police figured out that since I decided not to work with them to find Dank, I was going to seek my own justice. They were almost right, but not quite. I had too much going for myself and wasn't going to screw that up for a nickel and dime hustler.

My only reasoning behind dropping the charges was that I knew the streets well enough to know that if there's anyone with as many enemies as Dank, the streets were going to deal with him eventually. It would be a lie to say he never crossed my mind. In fact, the incident haunted me in the form of nightmares and daydreams for months, but the devil is a liar.

SEVENTEEN

REDEEMED

In reflecting back over my life up to this point, the choices I made definitely played a major role in my "exile" season. It all began that night (to be exact) I called my beloved mother out of her name and used the "B" word instead. As it says in the Bible, Exodus 20:12 (KJV) *"Honor thy father and thy mother: that thy days may be long upon the land which the LORD thy God giveth thee."* . . . I opened a portal; in fact, I blew the door wide open to wreak havoc in my life. This portal was one that only God Himself could shut only after I begin to repent and ask my mom to forgive me. I decided to stay prayed up saying prayer after prayer at home and at church. For a while, I convinced myself that I was possessed by demonic spirits based on the kind of nightmares I had. As a result of that, my prayers increased and I asked God specifically to give me back my peace of mind, wisdom, knowledge, and understanding. No wonder I kept going to church in Miami about thirty miles from my home in Palm Beach. If I had the option of being rich beyond my wildest dreams with sleepless nights, or being poor with good rest, the latter would win any day.

As it was, good rest was going to take a while as the pressure to get me into the police station intensified. Different POs would come by our home armed at all times of the night asking my folks where I was (they normally never come armed or after sundown). There was no warrant so they couldn't send a police officer. Since I reported for the month already, they couldn't force me to come in again. The heat was too much, so to cool things down, I finally called the detective, Detective Vunrie. She was a rookie female officer that didn't want the case because there was no evidence pointing to me except hearsay, according to my lawyer. Being that Delray Beach was a small town, it was common for cases to be based on rumor.

We set up a time and I showed up with my sister. We both were understandably nervous; being that it was my first time in an interrogation. I smoked a cigarette like it was the last one on earth before walking into the police station. My lawyer at the time, Erick Dutch, wanted to charge me $300 to speak on my behalf at the interrogation. I thought the price was outrageous, especially with school only a week away. He was going to tell them that I wouldn't answer any questions; I could do that myself. You can bet your bottom dollar that's what I did.

Being an individual with a felony record, I was taught a thing or two from my jailhouse lawyers and years of watching Court TV (now called Tru T.V.) shows about the judicial system. I knew I didn't have to come in for questioning, but it was necessary in order for them to rule me out as a suspect, if at all' I did it so they would call the dogs off. I took it very personal when they kept stinking up my home with their presence looking for me. My mom and sister were strong for me. I love them even more for their support in the matter. The funny thing was that my early termination of probation hearing

The Courage To Believe

was coming up in two months, so things had to be smooth with the PO in order for the judge to put my freedom papers in my hands. I couldn't be a suspect in a murder investigation and think the judge wasn't going to consider keeping shackles on me until I was cleared. At this point, it wasn't looking too good for me with all the publicity about the case.

Kerlene drove me to the station and we prayed together in the lobby. After about 10 minutes of waiting, the detectives showed up, but wouldn't let my sister into the interrogation room with me. Kerlene gave me extra strength by advising me to just tell them the truth and that she will be waiting on me. Here I am, sitting in this conference room with two detectives playing the good cop bad cop routine. The interrogation room didn't look like the ones on TV where it's small, cold, and impersonal. This room was pretty nice with a beautiful round, wooden table. Being a member of the student government, I could recognize a conference room when I saw one. Perhaps they wanted to make me feel comfortable so I could spill the beans that I really didn't have. The woman detective asked me a couple of questions for the record like my name and address etc... I couldn't believe that I was actually sitting in an interrogation room and, for a few minutes, all their words sounded like gibberish!

For a moment, my mind went through a flashback episode of when I was in elementary school. In the third grade, I was accused of stealing a teacher's purse by two students I didn't know. Two things were wrong about that picture. First of all, I never stepped into this teacher's classroom before.

Second, I was such a shy kid at the time that it was completely out of character for me to do such a thing. After three days of interrogations in the principal's office with all the parents present except mine, a verdict was accomplished. I was free from the tales those students told. To make a long story short, the two students that accused me were caught with the purse a week later after buying the whole neighborhood ice cream.

I snapped out of it, she proceeded to ask me if I knew a person by the name of Ron McNeil.

I said, "No, I don't, ma'am."

"Are you sure you don't know Ron McNeill?" the other detective asked me rudely.

I moved towards the microphone on the table and repeated, "No, I don't know any one by the name of Ron."

His face turned bright red and if the situation wasn't as serious as it was, I would've laughed in his face; this definitely wasn't a laughing matter. I didn't want to give them any space or room to come up with a conclusion that I had any part of the crime at hand.

This whole time, I'm sitting down calmly with my hands under the round table, shaking like a prostitute in church.

"What does this Ron McNeill have to do with me?" I asked.

She says, "Ron was the real name of Dank, the person who stabbed you last year." She added, "He was shot a couple of days ago."

"So that's why I'm in here," I replied, "because I'm a suspect of shooting some one that stabbed me a year ago?"

They thought they were slick. I knew he was killed; the whole town knew, but they kept saying he was shot in hopes that I would incriminate myself by saying I didn't "kill" him. Instead, I said that I didn't know about any shooting.

At this point, I was extremely uncomfortable in their presence because I peeped what trick they were playing with me. Yeah, I knew he was killed just like everyone else did. A small town like that, word gets around super quick and even faster when a murder is involved. I told the detectives that I wasn't going to answer any more questions without my lawyer present. The bad cop really didn't like that.

He says to me, "You are not even a suspect and you want to get all defensive crying for a lawyer."

"First of all, I'm not crying for a lawyer because my family has one retained that is working for us on other legal matters," I replied.

That reason was for Pharo, my little brother's case.

"Secondly, I don't trust the cops after one of you punched my mom in the chest, knocking her to the ground." I continued, "I am a black man with a bright future and using an attorney wouldn't be so bad, so why not use him?"

As soon as I said that, I got up saying, "Sorry, but I'm not answering anymore of your questions. If you have any more questions, please ask my attorney."

I left my lawyer's card on the table and walked out. To be honest, I was very brave to go there not knowing if they were going to arrest me or not. All I could do was clear my name and if telling the truth was going to lock me up, then so be it. Last time I checked, God didn't like ugly. Whatever happened to Dank, that's between him and God. May he rest in peace. It was only my faith that walked me out of that room handcuff free.

I was so deep into this interrogation nightmare that I forgot they couldn't stop me from leaving. I ended the interrogation the way I did because I know how cops work. They would've taken something little that I said out of context and bring it to the state attorney and would've eventually got a warrant for my arrest. They probably only had their eyes on me because rumors of our so-called beef. Leaving the police station was when the reality that my freedom could be in jeopardy dawned on me. I couldn't be their piñata because I had a future to catch up with and sitting in jail for a year or two fighting a murder charge didn't sit too well with me; so I decided to go into exile until my lawyer found out what was going on. It was my attorney Eric's idea to do so in the first place. My concern was that it was going to make me look guilty by hiding; however, Eric made me realize that there was no warrant for my arrest, so it was perfectly legal to lay low while he did his job. Our home was under around-the-clock surveillance and the detectives came by harassing my family on a regular basis. It was time for me to go far enough to get away, but close enough to get a sense of the situation.

I went into exile in Miami-Dade County and stayed with some of my family I hardly knew, but had heard of. When most people think of Miami, they think about fun in the sun and sexy people. That wasn't the case at all. My cousins Noel and François were brothers who took me under their wings. These guys were the black sheep of the family and were always out of town on the cash route. At one point, they were worth a little over two million from a heist they pulled on a drug stash house. Wherever they were posted up in a club eventually turned into the V.I.P. section. People would just flock to them as if they were celebrities, but they were "hood-stars." These brothers were always well dressed and had clean haircuts with flamboyant, platinum neck chains and watches flooded with real diamonds. It seemed as if everybody in Miami knew them because we never paid to get into any club, and had no trouble going backstage at concerts to discuss business with some of the biggest rap artists in the business. They had a connection to everything and anything. Their friends, male and female alike, all drove expensive foreign cars. I didn't think that being in exile was going to be this much of a showcase, but hey, this was Miami.

Redeemed

It wasn't the best feeling being away from home, but given the situation, it was definitely necessary. All this was going down during Hurricane Katrina; while everyone was panicking about hurricane preparation, my mind was someplace else. School had started, but they took a two-week break because the campuses in South Florida were in chaos due to Katrina. Trees, dirt, and debris made the schools hazardous, but this was good news for me because I was already missing classes that fall semester. Hurricane Katrina bought me time to think of my next move.

Plans were being made for me to leave the states for Haiti or one of the Caribbean Islands until things cooled down. If I wasn't a strong believer in God as my Lord and Savior, I would've taken that trip. In no time, I became a bible reading fanatic because I just didn't know what to do. No one's advice made sense to me, however the messages from the Bible did. I was so stressed out by the situation that I could not read the writing on the wall, which was plain and simple: *Ask God for wisdom.* My mom, being highly religious, gave me a fairly large old black Bible to read, knowing that I didn't have mine with me. That was the best gift she had given me other than birth. I just needed a sign from above on what to do. The main thing was to maintain my spirituality and mental strength during that time which had its ups and downs. I couldn't remain one-dimensional despite my problems. My mind was spinning endlessly with thoughts like a quarter on a glass table. One of my family members came to me with a proposition of paying a witch doctor to do some voodoo to get rid of this problem, in other words, her advice was to sell my soul to the devil. Without any hesitation, I told her that God is the only answer, and I would never ... ever sell my soul or worship satan for anything in this world!

Finally, the Lord told me to continue the mission of finishing school through a dream: I was in a classroom with my hand raised to ask the professor a question with a huge smile. It was from that dream I understood I was to go back to school. It wasn't going to be easy. The routine was very grueling: (1) I would wake up 5 a.m. Monday through Thursday to catch a bus after a mile walk with a seven pound backpack to the bus stop, (2) I'd hop on a train leaving Miami on 79th street that I would miss if I didn't run immediately 50 yards to the train station after getting off the bus, (3) take another bus to get me to BCC (Broward Community College) where I took French I and II, (4) after that, I would take a bus back to the Tri-Rail train station heading north to the Boca Raton train station, and, (5) in Boca, I'd hop on a bus that would take me to FAU. My professors understood my tardiness for the most part; however, I had no control of the punctuality of the trains and buses. Eventually, I caught earlier trains just to make it on time. Heading back to Miami was much easier with one straight shot down south. Surprisingly, I did this for an entire semester.

This whole time, I ignored the fact that I was on probation because the decision was made that I would turn myself in during the Christmas break. A warrant for my arrest was certain due to neglect of not reporting, but I wasn't in a rush to go back in. There was nothing the system could do to me that they haven't done already except for prison. As I was praying, I realized my success would get my family to another level and with God's help, to another dimension.

There was a rumor amongst my family that there is a curse or subliminal chains holding us back from increasing in life financially and spiritually. Straight out the womb, we constantly struggled and still are for the most part... scratching our heads with one hand while with the other hand we were crossing our fingers to pay the bills or to achieve some kind of substantial success such as graduating from college, owning homes, or having a professional career.

My Pastor at the time, Verna DuPont (New Beginnings Ministries), once said that many families have generational curses on them and the evidence is in the way we were raised. As it was, my family was not thinking beyond the box or of our current and past situations. Most black families aren't taught life skills such as saving our money, self-respect, and morale, but we are taught certain lessons to help us survive which was only half the battle. Pastor DuPont was right I wasn't taught how to balance a check book, how to invest, how to sacrificially save. Living with my family in Miami confirmed that some kind of negative spirit was roaming free amongst my family. They had jobs, but were living in a third world environment. No one was supporting the other which was the only tradition we have... an "all about me" attitude. The level of ignorance was astounding with regard to blessing or assisting another relative that could break the chain, ultimately taking our family to another level.

The Courage To Believe

While on exile, I was able to contemplate several important variables in my life as well as in the lives of the rest of my family. There are two houses in America that are owned within my family of twenty-eight adults. Three cars are newer than 2001. One person has a bachelor's degree (me) and one successful marriage out of 17 first generation adults in the country over the age of 21. The feeling of shame came upon me and I wanted to break this trend, this lack of achievement and support of one another. But the question remained, what was holding my family back in such a way for generations? Regardless of this dilemma, I was determined to do something about it. Education and entrepreneurship was the best way to do it.

I took a wide range of courses, but the one that stood out the most was African Studies. The class seemed like a woman's course because there were about forty students and only three of us were male. It was very informative on the continent of Africa as a whole. I learned that Africa's map had 61 countries, about the pre and post-colonial history of different regions, and how beautiful the people were before foreign powers separated the "Mother Land." The most significant project I've done throughout my educational journey was when I received an assignment to pick the country in Africa we found most interesting and present it to the class. Our professor Dr. Beokubits gave me Benin, Africa to conduct my research and do my presentation on due to the fact we had a discussion earlier in the semester about the roots of Haitian slaves. With my Haitian heritage, my professor sensed that this would serve me good to study my ancestors.

The professor truly believed my ancestors mainly came from the country currently known as Benin, formerly known as Dahomey. It's located in Western Africa next to Nigeria. I was extremely proud that Benin was once home to a "Warrior Kingdom" that lasted 200 years (17th to the 19th century) until a second war invasion (Benin won the first battle) of Portuguese and French soldiers outnumbered the African army (Kneib). They separated and conquered the land, turning everyone that didn't flee the land into slaves and shipping them to the Caribbean Islands; mainly to the island of Saint Domingue. The only reason why Dr. Beokubits and other scholars believe Benin was the home of Haitian ancestry is because they practiced Vodun (Voodoo) heavily. The fact of the matter is most of the western coast of Africa practiced Voodoo as a religion daily.

During all of this intellectual awakening in school, I had a dark cloud over my head. I still had to take care of the probation situation. The sad part was that I violated the terms of my probation and had to turn myself in. Turning myself in wasn't hard for me to do, especially since it eventually had to be done. At the time, I stepped away from Baby Cakes because of the stress and didn't want to drag her into my whirlwind. I really loved this girl and I did not think any other woman (except for my mother) could or would love me as hard as she did. Baby Cakes was loyal, but young with a lot of growing up to do especially with five years between us.

Before going in, I hooked back up with Queta since she knew a bit about the law and dealt with lawyers. We wanted to

The Courage To Believe

see if we could rekindle the old flames we passionately had once upon a time. She did not completely know the throes of chaos that I've been in or was going to be in. By this time, Queta was a grown woman with her bachelor's degree in business, a full-fledged body with plenty of assets top and bottom, and a career just like she always planned. After a few conversations and romantic dates together, we started right where we left off years ago. The only difference is that we started smoking weed together. Guess it was a habit she picked up at FSU. I told her what time it was with the PO violation and she was down with it, but Baby Cakes was still in my heart.

With the intelligence and financial means of Queta, I felt more comfortable with her being my eyes and ears on the street than Baby Cakes. Her house phone didn't accept collect calls, but Queta's phone did (a crucial tool being locked up). One day I slipped up by telling both women to come visit me, but couldn't reach either one in time to cancel. This was a big problem in the visitation area. When the guard asked me which one to allow in the visitation room, it was a question I didn't want to answer because no matter whom I chose, somebody was going to be extremely hurt. Since Queta was quarterbacking my defense on the streets and had the financial means to fight for me, I chose *her*. Keep in mind that there was a possibility that I wasn't going to be released due to my suspected involvement in a shooting. Baby Cakes let someone hold her car that day, so she had to catch a bus in the pouring rain back home miles away. I felt really bad when she told me that. Baby Cakes was there for me through a lot of bad times and I let Queta come back into my life without any regards for

Baby Cake's feelings. The decision during that visitation was one of three regrets in my life that I've ever had to live with other than leaving the University of South Dakota.

     Nonetheless, I was released on Christmas Eve at four in the morning one week after turning myself in. I remember being so happy and thrilled to be home for Christmas, just like in the movies, except this was real life…*my* life. With all of the worrying and stress from the PO, detectives, and jail…it felt like the world was lifted off of my shoulders in one night. My guilt for neglecting Baby Cakes wouldn't allow me to continue with Queta, so I ended up without either of them and was single again.

EIGHTEEN

MATING SEASON

Every relationship is different even though similarities are always there. Personally, I have had an array of good and bad experiences in this arena and these "interviews" definitely gave me insight as to what comprises a soul mate. At inception of a possible new friendship and/or relationship, it is inevitable that both parties will be mindful to only put their best foot forward, keep in mind that hidden in the back, in the corner, in the dark is the other foot which is usually deformed. Let's be honest, we all have old baggage that must be unpacked and dismantled before starting any new relationship. As the friendship is being cultivated into a possible relationship and quality time is being spent together, once the trust factor appears, the deformed foot will slowly draw closer to the light. At this exposure, we make a conscious decision to continue seeing each other or to move on to the next meeting. I frequently say to myself that if I could take a piece from every woman I've ever dated, I could put together the perfect companion. What we, including myself, fail to realize is that we'll never have the perfect mate because we will always find imperfect flaws within each other. It's the imperfections that make us beautiful and our differences that make us unique.

By the age of 27, I had been in love twice. However, there was one relationship that I learned the most from as an adult; she was a tough cookie, and thrifty with how she spent her money. Her name was Katurah Gilbert, a bookkeeper. I met her through an associate when I was looking for a bookkeeper for the club events I was hosting. I took her to lunch a few times to discuss business, but somehow we started to get a little personal. She was cute, independent, and single, so I went in for the hunt of love. Katurah revealed to me that she found me very attractive, but didn't like mixing business with pleasure. Eventually, our meetings became more about pleasure than business, which was cool with me. Keeping a balance between the two came easy to me.

I admired her fashion style, the way she kept her house clean, and her respect for money. She taught me how to catch a penny before it hit the ground, a real life leprechaun. Sound investments, saving money, and tracking every dollar spent was the bottom line when it came to finances. We had an interesting relationship because she wasn't your typical black woman. She had a rebuttal for every thought, idea, or statement I had which got to be a little annoying. Everybody's different, but she was unique in her own secret world. From the outside looking in, she looked like the perfect woman, but she had a circle of scandalous friends; most were involved with credit, real estate, and investment scams. If you weren't part of their circle, then you were just a text buddy if you were lucky. Katurah would actually keep her phone on a contact list only, which means, if your name wasn't saved in her cell phone your call would go straight to voice mail. I always felt she was foolish for that, what if someone had an emergency and lost their phone?

The Courage To Believe

Some of her friends were also swingers, which was a new world to me. I've always known what it meant to be a swinger, but had never been exposed to this world of money, greed, and lust. We were invited to a club in Ft. Lauderdale called Scampy's, a swingers club. At the time, I wasn't a full-time Christian, so we didn't really know what we were getting ourselves into. Most of the people were white with a few Hispanics, and a couple of blacks. Everyone had to bring in their own bottle to drink (to guarantee that you got drunk I suppose or maybe they had no liquor license). We didn't partake in any of the group activities, but we did observe and eventually enjoyed ourselves in private. But, watching these people, it looked so evil to me how everyone was nude without a care in the world. At one point, we were in a dim, red room all by ourselves kissing and drinking. Next thing we knew, the room was filled with people and it looked literally like snakes in the grass coiling and mating. I just got this negative vibe from that experience and it was time for us to go. We should have never entered that place. Not sure what I was thinking, but it's a perfect example of how friends or even friends of friends can influence your life.

Money brought us together and I'm surprised that it didn't break us apart. Females today just want an ambitious companion because they are ambitious themselves and don't want a man that's always in their pocket. The beginning of our relationship was full of mental dogfights. She was the Yorkie with a red ribbon on top while I was the Doberman with a blue necktie. We argued continuously, trying to get each other to listen; we were the black version of "Mr. and Mrs. Smith." The makeup sessions were unbelievable, but we both agreed that we weren't made for each other. By forcing our compatibility, the truth was bound to be exposed.

Even though it was mutually beneficial for us to remain together financially, we both knew deep down inside we wouldn't last. The respect factor wasn't there. She acted as if she bought my privacy, self-respect, and with them, my pants. She was a decent cook, supportive, and kept her life in order. I yearned for a companion that was business oriented and good with money, and I got what I asked for—so I thought.

I must've been pretty confused until I realized it was not Katurah or anyone else who has helped me along my journey; it was my Father up above, guiding His son through the battlefields providing directions, signs, food, shelter, and positioning me with good people. Other than love, the survival of my genes with the optimal companion, the mother of my children, and territorial gains, is what life with a wife pretty much comes down to. Once upon a time it was impossible for me not to pursue every fine woman that crossed my path. After enough dating, I've come to realize women are expensive and the more women I dated, the more unnecessary stress I was forcing upon myself. Men, including myself, need an ambitious woman with many attributes to bring to the table.

I'm tired of these "interviews" with fake smiles and phony interests. Tired of rain checks and getting stood up. The fact that I am not a bad looking guy I could only imagine how many times other guys get stood up. I wanted more; no more lowering my standards for temporary pleasure. Is it wrong to want to be treated like a "king?" If I can't treat my woman like a queen, then it's no fun. That's only possible if we're on the same page and she reciprocates. All I want from a companion is for her to be a God-fearing Christian, smart, beautiful, loves kids, is lady-like, ambitious, has a nice backside, shapely legs, has that ghetto-with-class demeanor, honorable, open-minded, respectful, stylish, wears her natural hair most of the time (there's nothing wrong with weave as long as you're not wearing it 365 days a year), and let's not forget to mention, knows how to cook. That's all. Are these standards too much to ask for? Now, you may think that sounds like a lot, but to me, a pancake isn't a pancake if you leave out the milk.

The thought has occurred that I may never find my soul mate by being so picky. Perhaps these standards are a bit much, but why settle for anything but the best? Having faith will be the only way to receive such a treasure as a good wife. We want the right person for right *now*, but God gives us that person who will be there for us down the road. Finding a mate based on what we can see is dangerous because it is what we can't see that does the most damage; things like diseases, secrets, and hidden motives. Now, some may ask what I have to offer. That's a legitimate question and here are my answers: I'm a God-fearing man, smart, handsome, a gentleman, love kids, ghetto-with-class, ambitious, open-minded, respectful, stylish, physically fit, and traditional, a protector, honorable, organized, a business man, and a future multi-millionaire.

Relationships are competitive today. I wouldn't doubt that it has always been that way. You must be financially stable yourself to have a seventy-five percent chance of hooking up with a financially stable partner of the opposite sex or vice versa, according to the secular world. A broke person most likely will be with a broke mate because they both think broke. To be in the same environment of some people, (e.g. celebrities), you have to spend time and/or money to place yourself in their popular surroundings. It could be at a ball game, V.I.P. at a club, a tennis match or even a title-boxing match. The best place to meet a Christian woman would be at church, but don't let that fool you, because many people are fronting to live "holier than thou." Still, I would take my chances.

What's the difference between a female and a lady?
A lady is a female with dignity.

It is so funny how our two genders are confused on whether or not they are a lady or gentleman. It's more than just diamonds, pearls, a suit, or a dress and makeup that determine whether someone has class. My presence here on earth didn't take place around the roaring twenties, revolutionary 60's, or the hip 70's when everyone understood order. Husband and wife, man and woman, ladies and gentlemen ... today's dating scene is a joke. It seems as if everyone is trying to have sex on the double or attempting to see what they can get out of the other person. Many people don't even know the person's last name they are sleeping with. It's a challenge to even be a complete *gentleman* because the average female won't let men do the simplest things for them. A vast majority of women want to be both the man *and* the woman in the relationship. To make matters worse, there are men who aren't sure of their masculine gender.

What's the difference between a female and a lady? A lady is a female with dignity. Try opening a door for a female and see if she'll let you. Half the time it's impossible because she has already beat you to the door instead of easing back a bit. Try pulling a chair out at a restaurant for your female acquaintance and see what happens. Times have really changed. Decades of single mothers taking on the responsibilities of both sides of parenthood have led to a degree of independence that has transformed society for better or worse forever. In my opinion, I must admit that it has been for the worst with boys/men not having complete respect for women, even our mothers and sisters. A male figure doing his part in the home raising the kids together with the mother with love is a powerful component our world so badly needs. If I may add, black women, in particular, have definitely picked up their role since our men have been absent from home; however, our men are more present in the streets and in the prisons throughout the country. It irks me when I hear my friends and family that are incarcerated condone their illegal means of chasing money in the name of providing for their family.

I ask this question, "How can you provide for them now that you're locked up?"

I know in this world we have to provide, to protect, and to shelter our families. I understand this completely and it's the same with the wildlife out there in the jungle and forests—same principle. I so badly want our men to comprehend that those "Cowboy Days" are long gone. Technology has changed and the odds of getting caught doing any type of crime have greatly increased-especially if there are cameras around. With these smartphones you can have fifty cameras pointed at you to record or to snap a picture at any given time. A recorded bank robbery can be posted on YouTube, Facebook, and Twitter in a matter of seconds. If you have a woman, or anyone for that matter, that is pressuring you to get money and isn't encouraging you to get more interviews, then leave her expeditiously!

Morals and ethics have been replaced with currency. It's a psychological trend that has taken place mixed with the fear of being down, broke, and disgusted. The things that people are willing to do for money don't even surprise me anymore. In the history of the human race, sin has never changed, only technology has. Studying different cultures and political ideologies from all areas of the globe, I realize the lack of money/resources has a nasty effect on families, villages, communities, and nations. How else would people like Hitler, Pablo Escobar, Papa Doc and Edi Amin, come into power? They do it by promising a better life for their country with every intention to achieve their goals with violence.

The Courage To Believe

When all the chips are down and our backs are against the wall, it's our natural instinct to survive by any means necessary. Now here is the catch: that's what the devil wants - any means necessary. You are willing to sell your soul and join his staff of demons. Make no doubt about it —there is a "Battle of Good and Evil" taking place every day. If the devil can control the way you think, then he controls what you do since our actions are formed first as thoughts. I'm not telling you what I've heard. I'm telling you what I've lived!

I wish I had lived in primitive times when men only had to hunt down wild beasts and bring it home to his family. The man played a vital role in that era and understood that if he didn't bring home dinner, the household would starve. The woman also played a vital role if not a more significant one than the man by taking care of the children, the cooking, and the home. As society evolved, the gender roles gradually became altered. In the new millennium, women are the "Bread Winners" in most households for two reasons: 1) they are single parents, and 2) they are smarter in most cases from birth. I have no problem with my woman making more money than me because I'm neither a caveman nor egotistical. The fact of the matter is I am secure with the woman thinking that she's in charge. Today, a man has his work cut out for him. He must be able to be sensitive, a provider, a handyman, a protector, a lover, and a confidant. Instead of hunting down animals, we have to hunt down paychecks; however or whatever it takes to take care of the family.

"What is it that you do for a living?" has been the number one question of possible future companions for generations. Now that question has been replaced with, "What can you do for me?" Consciously or subconsciously, we all want a sense of security that our mate is financially secure or at least has some form of income. There was a time when this was asked indirectly with respect. Am I mad at this trend? No, but I am disappointed that the potential of a person is no longer valid consideration. I'll bet that women would have been more receptive of my interests if they knew I was writing a best-seller or had a multi-million dollar clothing line in the making...of course, not all women. There are women out there that don't allow cash to rule everything around them because the power of money is to be respected, not cherished. After all, money isn't the root of all evil, but the *love of money* is the root of all evil (1 Timothy 6:10; KJV). People who allow money to consume them while they think they are winning will actually sell their children, their bodies, their peace of mind, and even their souls.

When it is all said and done, human beings have the natural urge to gain power. There's some sort of primal urge to obtain as much power as our appetite can handle, and then some. When I say power, I mean the power to make people need us, want us, envy us. That's why there's a power struggle in most relationships, whether it be mother against father, sister against brother, husband against wife, teacher vs. student, neighbor vs. neighbor, criminals vs. cops, Clarence Thomas vs. Black America. Women in general are cool with the man wearing the pants, but there are times when a woman thinks she should be wearing the pants and not the other way around. This causes disorder, confusion, and shuts down the blessings of God.

NINETEEN

BIRTH OF AN ENTREPRENEUR

By 2005, I had faced way too many obstacles in my life for a young man, even though most came by way of the choices I made. Though my family may be small, we are very close and together we carry the strength of a battle tank. Family support is everything. Through thick and thin, we've been there for each other. That year I was determined to walk with my head up through the wind, water, and fire.

"I gotta make it, I gotta make it. I am going to make it!"

At this stage of my life, the scent of graduation was very close. I just had to stay on my feet and finish the race. I was graduating, but moving on to what? A bachelor's degree, along with hundreds of thousands around the country with the same degree or higher, plus a criminal record, which meant I was already losing in the job seeking rat race. I wished Kiyosaki's book "Rich Dad, Poor Dad" would've been brought to my attention years sooner. I was starting to miss the school life, and before entering the last semester, I already knew I had no idea what in the world I was going to do next.

History of the Caribbean was my favorite course due to the fact that it taught me so much about Haiti combined with what I already knew as well as how other countries in the Caribbean came to be. The more research I did on Haiti the more motivated I became to work harder. Haiti was once the number one producer of sugar in the world, on account of the people being forced to work 23 hour shifts (and we have the nerve to cry about nine hours of work)!

In my History of the Caribbean course, we had to produce a 15- page paper on a country of our choice (any country in the Caribbean). I chose Haiti since there was so much more I wanted to learn about my parents' homeland, especially about Toussaint L'Ouverture. I particularly wanted to know how he defeated the French and how he ended up in a French dungeon at Fort de Joux where he starved to death on April 7, 1803. After strenuous research, I found my answers in the original memoir of General Leclerc, a French soldier who actually set a trap for Toussaint and arrested him. The memoir was in French and I barely spoke any French, but my mom came to the rescue and we went over the general's diary word-for-word. She was excited to help me and I cherished her help since she couldn't help me with any of my homework growing up. The only thing we studied together as a family was the Bible.

There were times I would practically spend 10 to 12 hours on campus studying or researching. Of course, the classes and the library were not open for extended hours but, I was fortunate enough to have access to the keys of the Student Government office. Since I worked in S.G., the keys were issued to me, but I was breaking the rules of the building by staying so late. Only the S.G. President and Vice President could remain in the building after hours since they also had master keys to the building. I got into trouble once before when the fire alarm went off around 3:00 a.m. in the morning and a school campus officer escorted me out of the building. Even though the officials realized there wasn't a fire, I wasn't allowed to go back in. The officer asked me for my student ID and ran my name, and everything was okay; I knew I wasn't wanted for anything. The mere thought that I would probably lose my job for a careless act crossed my mind, so I stayed away from the office for a week until I realized the campus police never came to speak to any of my superiors.

Speaking of my superiors, I had no idea I was in the midst of baby sharks—the future leaders of America. All of the student government members were power hungry and in pursuit of positioning themselves comfortably in the real world. They already had their minds set on using student government as a platform to gain powerful affiliations with the sponsors of the university, resulting in great careers with excellent pay once they graduated. For example, Mr. Mratt, (former president of student government and the first black male president in 20 years) received a top marketing position for the Miami Heat. Olivia Kaun became President of a Fortune 500 company in New York. Everyone from the student government president to the event planner had bigger plans and I was just there to get a paycheck, oblivious to the power struggle between them. Two of the student government presidents during my tenure resigned after allegations of stealing funds of up to $500,000. It is not clear if the university filed charges on the two men. We were in charge of a $2,000,000 budget to disburse amongst the student organizations.

The Courage To Believe

Safe and secure is what I felt whenever I was on campus. I never felt threatened in any way once I was there; it was a safe haven for me. It was like being on another planet. Being in the streets always had me looking over my shoulder since I was living life in the fast lane. For that very reason, I could easily miss what was going on or know who was plotting against my future empire. On campus, that kind of nature didn't exist compared to what you'd find in the streets. Growing up, I always valued school in some way because it always proved beneficial to me in many forms. I can remember when I was 10 years old; I would constantly have late night nightmares. It would cause me to anxiously desire for the next morning to come. I literally would be up all night afraid to go back to sleep. I would keep my eyes wide open, zoomed in on the alarm clock like a sniper, eager to get ready for school, for the air conditioning and free food. School was a refuge. Growing up in the hood, we didn't have air conditioning in our home and we were very fortunate to have what my mom could put on the table for us to eat.

One thing I've been blessed to realize is that the stability of a person's home can make a significant difference in how successful or unsuccessful he or she will become. That's why the majority of folks in the ghetto never advance and it feels like a trap at times because of the instability of the home. With so many single parent homes, one can only wonder about the residual effects of slave history when slaveholders did not allow black slaves to get legally married. That's a very complicated psychoanalytical subject. For now, I'll just say the fortunate ones that have made it out of the ghetto, regardless of instability, are at times pulled back into the realism of the ghetto by many of our families' and friends' troubling situations. There's a great deal of negativity we attract. The conversations and engagements about drugs, police, sex, guns, and murder that took place in the ghetto exert a pull like magnets on a refrigerator. What kept our sanity were the many conversations about Black Jesus, children, home cooked meals, and most importantly, having the fortune of one day moving out of the ghetto. Having reserved time to reflect and a peaceful environment in which to think positively was something I lacked and pursued relentlessly. I needed to attract those two elements into my world if I was going to have the power to build an empire for my family and become the CEO of One Man Army, Inc.

I fought many battles, conquered several obstacles, and jumped countless hurdles to graduate college. It was a mission impossible. As a former track athlete, I was blessed to learn the elements of winning and finishing the race, no matter what. It wasn't easy, but with determination and faith, what could stop me other than myself? Through all the storms and many challenges in my lifetime, one of my dreams thus far came true. Kevin Dorival was somebody that day—a college graduate! I must say, wearing that cap and gown, I was as proud as a king walking to his throne after winning a long treacherous war.

The night before, I was out sinning and was drunker than Nick Nolte. My cousin Jon and I went to Club Boca Nights, a nightclub in Boca Raton, to celebrate. We had lots of drinks all night and were even permitted to walk into the club with our

The Courage To Believe

cups filled with Hennessy (but you did not hear that from me). My cousin was so drunk that he exposed his private to a drunk female while talking to her at the bar. He's from Miami and thought it was cool to do. The young lady threw her drink in his face and all over his shirt. I know it was only God that made us get home safe that night.

I was knocked out like a bear in hibernation in my soft bed. My phone was ringing all morning, but I had it on vibrate since the night after the club. If it wasn't for my friend Gar waking me up by talking on the Nextel walkie-talkie, I would've slept straight through my own college graduation.

All I heard on the walkie was, "I see you had a good time last night."

I jumped up and ran straight into the bathroom to take a quick birdbath, grabbed my cap and gown that I already had hanging over my headrest, and ran to my car half naked. Just kidding…but I did break every rule in the driving book that could've been broken that day. I ran stop signs, red lights, and on Interstate-95, I drove on the emergency lane all the way to the university's exit. Being late for my graduations seemed to be a trend since I was late for my high school ceremony also.

The graduation started at nine in the morning on May 15, 2005 and unfortunately, I woke up at 8:45 AM. I got there at 9:06 AM, which wasn't really that, bad, but I should've been there earlier. While on the way to the university's graduation, I briefly spoke to my sister over speakerphone and advised her to quickly talk to an official about my situation because I knew I had missed the sitting for the graduates.

My sister was able to get an administrator on the phone with me and they expressed that I, Kevin Dorival, was going to be escorted V.I.P. style during the ceremony. I was under the impression that I was the only one late, but after I sat down, five other graduates came in late as well. Seems like we all had hangovers because of the early celebrating we did the night before!

Every student was given six tickets and two extra if needed. I got eight tickets and gave them to my friends and family. Three people didn't show up, two brothers (actually none of my brothers could make it) and my mean grandmother who is actually much nicer now. I knew she wasn't coming because all my life she always doubted my siblings and me. So, it didn't surprise me when she didn't attend. The only reason I invited her was because, at the time, I was renting a back room at her house. She would promote every negative thing in the world, but missed this very positive occasion. I did however smile when I overheard her telling her friend I was graduating from college. My brothers not showing up hurt me a little. One thing I know for sure is, if my youngest brother, Pharo, wasn't in jail, he would've have been there because he is my biggest fan. My mom, two of my sisters, and two of my friends came to support me on that special day. It was like a thousand and one students that graduated that morning.

The Courage To Believe

All the many proud families and friends rooted for their loved ones; it was like magic. The Dean, Mr. Brogan, was telling heart touching life and death stories about a couple of the students that were very fortunate enough to graduate or to even be alive. Instantly, I began to think about the ups and downs, the ins and outs I had to overcome to get this degree...the times I was on exile, the weekly V.O.P. (violation of probation) vacations in jail, all the headaches I endured by moving from to house to house. I also thought about the people I knew personally that let life's circumstances get to them; circumstances that caused them to ultimately discontinue their education. I never wanted to be many things, but I definitely didn't want to be one of those students that never dropped back in after dropping out. It's true that, "The harder the struggle, the more glorious the triumph," (Swami Sivananda, a spiritual teacher).

Upon finishing school with a bachelor in politics (political science), I found myself in a temporary paradox. My past felony record wasn't going anywhere and I suffocated my future as a result of it, but was determined to breathe and exhale eventually. If only I reminded myself of the importance of walking straight and staying away from illegal activities. Teenagers know their records are cleared once they reach 18, but once you get to 18, everything sticks. There's no more day care at a detention center; its jail or prison. As I mentioned before, track & field taught me not to panic in close races—just relax and keep it moving forward. That's exactly what I practiced in life. The problem with the theory of not panicking is that it was a bit difficult to grasp at times, because keeping a roof over my head and amassing a growing debt made it difficult not to panic, which is only natural. Yes, there were many ways I could have gotten a quick few thousands of dollars, but it would have only caused me to succumb to my old ways. That's too easy and besides, I felt I had deserved and earned a better way to make a living. Why put everything I've worked so hard for on the line? And on top of that, I was beginning to love life again.

Of course, I anticipated that the hunt for a career in politics as an ex-felon was not going to be a walk in the park, but if I don't stand up for my community, then who will? It was a righteous cause, but what was underemphasized was how I was going to pay my bills. I paid close attention to the newspapers to see when politicians were going to be in town and eventually it paid off. Congressman Kendrick Meek was having a "Redemption Workshop" at a church in Liberty City, Miami. To find that church was another story because the street sign was destroyed by Hurricane Katrina. After driving around the neighborhood a few times, I noticed people walking toward a building, so I thought this had to be the place, and it was. Congressman Meek spoke with me briefly, exchanged business cards, and I handed him my resume. He told me to call him the following Tuesday, but I was never able to catch up with him again and quite frankly, never expected to. The workshop was being held for ex-felons wanting their civil liberties back (especially, voting rights). Mr. Meek is a politician, a successful black male, and I expected him to tell me whatever sounded good because the chances of us meeting again would be slim.

There was another politician in Miami that could have given me an opportunity to get my foot in the door. Arthur Teele was once a City and County Commissioner, as well as my sister's ex-boss. Unfortunately he fatally shot himself in the office building of the Miami Herald, the newspaper that was persecuting him literally with their articles about his career and personal life for years. They wrote articles regarding his alleged political corruptions to homosexuality; the latter levied by a convict in exchange for a lighter sentence. I really wish that he had not checked out in that fashion for my sake, also, since he was married and had a powerful position in Miami. For a black man in a city run by different ethnicities, Cubans and Jews, it was quite an accomplishment.

Through Mrs. Byrd, my guidance counselor, I met another important figure in the black community, Chief Braddock. Chief Braddock (Rev. Braddock) was a retired Miami-Dade Police Chief who moved to Broward County to minister at a Fort Lauderdale church. This dude had rank and was very active for a man of sixty years of age. When we first met, it was a privilege up until he said something that struck me as odd and out of line. We discussed my plan to start a staffing agency for ex-offenders to help them with job placements once they are released from jail or prison. Coincidently, the Chief was already in route for something similar. By the third time we met in 2005, he said, "You are a nobody trying to do business with people that are somebodies."

Needless to say, that was my last time in his office. I respected his stripes and experience, while I ignored that he was a grumpy, old man. He never knew he placed a dark cloud over my dreams. Dark clouds roll away eventually.

In need of a job, I took on a gig at a plastic factory—Flexal Packaging. Everyone around the way knew of someone that worked there. The pay was mediocre, but I took it at $10 an hour. It was a great company to work for since they gave many of us benefits. Most men, including myself, rarely had insurance or a 401(k). Flexal provided all of that and a sense of financial security...a critical component of manhood. When I heard that they hired a guy who just got out of prison for a home evasion, I knew instantly that I had a chance to get hired. There were three different 12 hour working shifts: A, B, and C. I worked C shift, which was from 7:00p.m. to 7:00a.m. on Mondays, Tuesdays, and Wednesdays. Every other Thursday, Friday, and Saturday I was off. Our shift never had to work on Sundays. The B shift worked on my days off. No one wanted the B shift since they always worked on boogie nights when everyone is out having fun on the weekends. B shift personnel always tried to transfer to C shift, but would rarely get the approval. B shift was especially tough for the guy with a girlfriend or a wife. The number one concern was whether or not their women were cheating on them while they were at work. Half the time, the women were practicing infidelity since their companion wasn't home when they were making their mating calls. Some of the guys would even pay someone to spy on their significant other.

The work wasn't difficult since the majority of the time we were sitting down packing plastic bags into boxes. Any given night, we would put together 200-300 boxes depending on the assigned station. It was our duty to prepare boxes for the next shift, which was shift A. Some stations (30 stations in total) did not require boxes at all. The machine would create a roll of plastic that could weigh as much 50 to 150 lbs. One or two stations required two or three guys to work them since the plastic rolls were massive. Each of these large rolls had to be weighed and placed on a crate, 6 ft. x 6 ft. 6 across and 6 ft. high. There were also smaller machines that spit out smaller rolls of plastic bags the size of toilet paper rolls. These were headaches since they usually messed up the most because of their rapid pace.

Staying up was the tough part during the 12 hours, but I learned quickly that there was ample time to read books while a couple of the other guys had their Bibles on hand. There were perhaps a total of 10 women that also worked in the factory; some of them did the same. I read mostly business books or business magazines such as Black Enterprise. I had no idea that black folks around the country were doing so well in the business world. Many of the articles were about entrepreneurs and CEO's of major corporations; they were making millions upon millions, or at the very least, a six figure income. This motivated me to pursue my dreams and to read with great earnestness while I worked hard. Also, I read many other types of books (all non-fiction) such as the autobiographies and biographies of A.G. Gatson, Malcolm X, Collin Powell, etc…My reading list also included books and magazines on marketing/promotions and web design. I could read a 300 page book in literally 2-3 days. In the 15 months I worked there, I

Birth of an Entrepreneur

feasibly read about 30 books on the clock. The supervisors never said anything to me until I obviously started a trend and everyone began reading books. They even banned books, but being rebellious, I continued to read if the station did not require my full attention. I felt like a slave being told I couldn't read. I understood that in order to change my future, I would have to acquire and apply knowledge that I gained from reading.

Ultimately, I went through a metamorphosis from a thug to a bookworm and into a handsome, businessman. I switched up my work uniform from wearing boots to wearing suits and ties. It was refreshing; a lifestyle of fine dressing that I've always enjoyed and also added to my physique. In order to dress for success, I would purchase a shirt, tie, and pants with every check to build up my wardrobe. On my days off, I would attend networking events or babysit my two nephews, Dave and D'ton Martimae. This was around the time I started my company, "One Man Army, Inc." which was incorporated as a promotions and marketing company. A revelation struck me when I was with my nephews one day. A way to make money while at the same time getting my name out there revealed itself... throw parties! My 26th birthday was coming up in a month, so I decided to throw a hotel party. I, One Man Army, Inc, hosted it. I received a little help from my cousin Cedrick. Immediately, I found out who made the best flyers and we went to work. I booked a hotel room at the Westin Hotel; the staff didn't know about the party, but it was going down anyway.

The Courage To Believe

I was determined to market my company. I wanted to get as many people to say or read OMA, Inc. at least once because the name is unforgettable. At this point, I really wasn't sure where I was going as far as the marketing of OMA, but I knew my people would support me. So, in the meantime, I was trying to make a name for myself not realizing that it was in the wrong way.

I found the strippers, cases of liquor (Hennessy and Grey Goose) and a D.J. Viola! Now, Friday the 13th had a lot of superstitious people scared to come out, but a lot of folks still showed up. I was so stressed out from doing everything from A to Z by myself, because it was hard to find help. About 50 to 60 people came, but most were females ready to jump into the pool and the Jacuzzi. A torrent of rain began to fall and lighting struck. The party was on the outside, but inside one of the rooms, I had two strippers shaking their tail feathers.

The game plan was to have the dancing outside and the private party in the room with the strippers; too much noise and weed smoking in the room caused the rooms next to ours to complain. Hotel personnel were pretty cool at first because I told them we were having a family reunion. But, there were one too many complaints about the gambling going on in the hallway and all of the shouting. This was a four star hotel, so I was expecting to get kicked out before 3:00 a.m. came around.

Passing out the hotel party flyers allowed me to meet other entrepreneurs along with business propositions. My next venture was at a strip club called "Synn Citi." This was an old club under new management in my hometown of Pompano Beach, FL. I came upon this club by an individual I knew of from FAU named Derrick. I never knew his name before, but recognized him from the dorms on campus. While I was passing out the "Off-Probation Bash" flyers on campus, he pulled me aside about a club proposition. A couple of weeks later, he called me to host a strip club with him on Thursdays, which became locally known as the infamous "Champagne Thursday's." At first, I was skeptical of doing business with him because I didn't know him from a can of paint, but the money was attractive and I needed the exposure for my company.

At the time, I was being forced out of my landlord's house because of an argument we had over $1,200 that I loaned her. I was barely getting hours at work, so I began hustling again to make ends meet. I moved in with my ex-girlfriend as a last resort. It took me a couple of days to get back to Derrick, but ultimately, I accepted the idea. February 16th was the kick-off date and the night was a success.

The turnout surprised the owner, Rodney, and his two managers. Hard work by two young men paid off. The bar and the dancers made plenty of cash that night and the Thursdays that followed. I had some wife-beaters air-brushed in different colors with One Man Army on them and rhinestone inlays. Some of the dancers wore these … real hot! All of the ladies wanted one, but they cost me about $20 each. I knew that I stumbled on a gold mine at this point. My reputation in Pompano and Fort Lauderdale moved up escalator style.

The Courage To Believe

Everyone knew me as One Man Army while some called me "One Man" or "Army." I observed that everyone had smiles when the cash was flowing and friendships were made with money as the glue. Once the cash stopped coming in, friends disappear and smiles turn into middle fingers.

My hustle was going well and decent enough that I was able to save money to hire a celebrity to perform at the club. The opportunity came when I met J.T. Money in Miami at a concert at the Orange Bowl. He was on stage performing with Rick Ross (before he became popular), and when everyone got off stage, I stepped to J.T. (Two hit singles, Hit'em High and No Problems). I wasn't nervous, but I wasn't my usual cool either since it was my first time speaking to a rap star or any celebrity in a long time. I gave him my club flyer and asked him if he could come and perform at the club. He wasn't planning on being in town, but would be if the price was right. So, while we exchanged numbers, my Blackberry went blank making me look like an amateur. J.T. took my number and said that he was going to call me. I thought he surely wouldn't because 90 percent of the people in the entertainment business are full of it. He called me within 48 hours of our initial conversation.

My partner didn't want to put up any money for J.T. because he felt that he could get someone better to perform and for free. Of course he never did. So, I made the J.T. show happen. I only had five days to let as many people as I could know that he was going to be performing for the first time in Pompano Beach. I ran around like a chicken with its head cut off. The bulk of the work was done over the air on underground radio stations that were up and running at the time. The club was packed to capacity with exotic dancers, clubbers, both male and female.

At the end of the night, I collected the money, but my partner wanted half. That was normal; however that night wasn't the usual since he didn't put in one dollar for the promotion costs or the artist fees. At the door, we collected about $5,000 and it was only fair that I take over fifty percent of the net profit after paying the artist, D.J., and security. This caused a big argument and from then on, I couldn't trust him and did not shake his hand again. It's a shame, because it was a great partnership up until that point, but it is what it is.

"Champagne Thursdays" forged right ahead as usual, but was slipping from the normal numbers that we were used to getting. It doesn't take a genius to figure out that the less people that walk into the club, the less money will be made at the bar. Money stayed on my mind like white on rice. I had other plans to make more money, but would cost more than I've ever had. Just having voluptuous, black women dancing wasn't adding up and the missing ingredients were a larger venue and a hotter rap star. The club had to be Joseph & Joey's.

Club Joseph & Joey's was the only large venue that was giving black promoters an opportunity to do business. Just like Synn Citi, Club Joseph's mainly wanted 100% of the bar money while the promoters get the money collected at the door. As any business person would know, the real money is at the bar.

The Courage To Believe

A club the size of Joseph's can hold eight hundred legally but can take about 1,200 people that will drink some sort of liquor nine out of nine times. That's roughly $20,000 if everyone spends about $15 at the bar. Need I say more?

The next step was to find a partner that was willing to go half on the project with me. I found that partner in D.C. of Dollarz and Centz Entertainment, a local rap entity. D.C. and I decided we would get B.G. (Bling Bling was his most popular song) of Chopper City Records to come down and perform. We had an idea of the amount of stress and the crap that came with the territory of shows, but nothing prepared us for Pretty Boy and West. These two individuals were brought to the table because they had done plenty of shows at Club Joseph's and could teach us the ropes. With intelligence and tenacity, all they had to do was show me the boxing arena and I'd fight my way through.

Getting B.G. wasn't difficult at all, because we used our connections to get to him and his management. That was a big mistake because that just made his price higher as if we were in bidding war against each other. The final price was $14,000 for May 7, 2006 and we could have booked him for $10,000. Ouch! This didn't just make me want to kick myself in the head, but this was a mistake that would cost us dearly in the end. We slit our own throats at the beginning of the race and we knew it. The key to the promotion game is to spend as little as possible so that you can break even faster. The duo decided that we would split the cost; they pay for the club, hotel,

Birth of an Entrepreneur

limousine, food, and the airline tickets, while we pay for the artist.

The duo already had a show going down on Easter Sunday at Club Joseph's with T.I. and his Pimp Squad Click (PSC). Now, I understood that this was going to be a huge event for them and for everyone that was going to be in the club that night. I also understood that the duo wasn't going to have too much time to sit down and go over everything with us, but they only made the attempt once. We would have meetings scheduled and they wouldn't show up or even call for a rain check. What really broke the camel's back was when we had a meeting planned to go over the flyers, amongst other things, and only West showed up. Pretty Boy told me he was at a beauty salon with his girlfriend getting her hair done. To top that off, he said, "She has one more track left to do in her hair and I'll be on my way." It was obvious that he was incompetent and we no longer wanted to continue doing business with either of those two, even though Pretty Boy was just one of the partners. Anyway, May 7th was a month away and they still didn't have the club booked.

Because of all of these raggedy edges, I called the club behind the duos back and had a meeting set up with one of the managers. The duo told us that the club wouldn't allow new promoters to rent the club, but that turned out to be a lie because they wanted a piece of our action. They told us bits and pieces of what goes on when presenting a proposal before they realized the show was going on without them. With the information that I gathered from West, I typed up my own proposal and presented it to the club manager, Steven, with $1,500 cash in an envelope. A deal was struck with the club and our "John Hancock's" were on the dotted line. It was going down. That was a big relief and a load off our shoulders because it could have turned out differently. If we couldn't get the club that night we would be in big trouble due to the fact that B.G. already had half of his money that was non-refundable.

Finally, we got the ball rolling. The half-page glossy flyers went into production, which cost us about $700 for 10,000 of them. We had the radio commercials made that were aired on every local, underground radio station from Delray to South Beach and one mainstream station, 103.5 "The Beat" which costs $1,100 by itself alone. A BET commercial was also aired at the price of another $1,200 or so. Our goal was to make sure that everybody and their baby momma knew that B.G. was going to be in Ft. Lauderdale thanks to Dollarz and Centz and hosted by One Man Army, Inc.

From the starting blocks, this event was a rollercoaster and it was my first, major account as a promoter. I had to get my cherry popped and B.G.'s management made sure of that; his booking agency worked with me to get the airline tickets and a few minor things. The representative I worked with was Hillary. This woman was what you would call a female pit-bull in a skirt. No one was able to get to me over the phone the way she did. Hillary was just supposed to get the plane tickets, but she ended up hustling an extra two grand out of our pockets.

She had the tongue of Medusa and she drove us crazy with her powerful phone conversations. This lady was good.

The flyers had a B.G. picture on the front and a smaller one on the back where we also tagged an invitation for an "Off House Arrest" block party at Apollo Park. At the bottom was a small picture of the artist leaning on a banner stating that the after party was at Club Joseph. Would you believe that this woman threatened to sue us and cancel the show for false advertisement? She felt we were advertising that he would be at the park. It was plain to see that she was fabricating a story and it seemed like a routine scheme. The suit would be dropped if we paid their camp an unspecified amount to show up at the block party. On top of that, she wanted us to pay $350 for B.G. to do a radio drop, (a five second or shorter radio commercial) when radio drops to promote the event were usually free of charge.

Hillary knew that we were rookies and she was taking every advantage of what she perceived to be our naiveté. However, she underestimated just how much of a hustler I was and still am. We were forced to find an entertainment lawyer, Joan F., who was a great asset to us in dealing with Hillary and anything that had to do with the show. The extra $2,000 for the block party appearance was a battle that would have to be fought in a courtroom after the show because the timing was too delicate for legal threats. They didn't want to cancel the show and risk getting sued by us just as much as we didn't want to get sued by them.

The Courage To Believe

    The day B.G. dialed D.C.'s phone to leave a message for our radio commercial, he was calling the wrong number. I gave Hillary two different cell phone numbers but she, somehow, gave him the wrong number. She ended up blowing up my phone while I was in a meeting with the club owner regarding some disagreements with a new contract his manager tried to make me sign. I never looked at the phone to see that it was Hillary calling me out of respect for the meeting; I didn't pick up or even look at my phone, which was on, vibrate. The owners of the club were rumored to be mob-related. Perhaps it was because they are Italian, always dressed in all black, and drove all black Mercedes. It was an honor on my part to finally meet them.

    I just couldn't comprehend why she didn't have him call my phone for the commercial. We ended up waiting another 10 days before the artist would give us that commercial in order to meet our pre-sale ticket quota. I'm quite sure he's a busy man, being that he has reached platinum status in the rap game, but you would think that he would find 30 seconds to leave a message for someone who paid him a $7,000 deposit.

    Meanwhile, D.C. was waiting on his newborn to be delivered. The baby was due any day now, and I told him that I bet that we would get the radio drop the day his baby boy was born. Guess what? That's exactly what happened on Friday, the 28th of April. Adon was born and we got the call later the same night. I was nearly hysterical when I got the call from D.C. telling me to listen to the drop. I wasn't sure what he had me listening to, but when I realized that it was B.G.'s voice on the voicemail, I went berserk. Hip Hip Hooray!

I'm really not that emotional over good or bad news, but the message verified one thing we had been trying to figure out for a month—whether the show was going down and it was! There's a lot of shady promoters in South Florida and only a handful of them that give the people what they want. Since the T.I. show was a fluke that left about 1,500 people enraged, the burden of proving to club goers that the B.G. show was legit was on us. As soon as I got the drop, I went to different hoods, blocks, salons and barbershops playing the message to the doubters and supporters. We were selling V.I.P. wristbands at $50 a pop and I sold at least 40 of them from the voice message alone.

A lot of doubters and haters along with so-called friends came along with this show. The most popular rumor was that we didn't have the money to have B.G. perform. That only motivated me. I'm a true believer that when people hate on you, it's a good thing. I can't speak for D.C., but I couldn't afford to have paid for B.G. to perform on my own. Cutting out the duo was going to cause us to put up a lot more cash than expected. Originally, May 7th was just supposed to introduce us to the club promotion game, but we had an opportunity to make a lot of cash if we cut out the middleman.

I tried to get some sponsors with a packet that an associate gave to me, but was unsuccessful in getting any until I had a flat tire. Yeah, the revelation of how to pull in sponsorship intersected with the moment in time the flat tire happened. The idea hit me to ask the owner of a tire shop, which was a very nice woman, Mrs. D. She told me she believed in helping others and gave me a generous amount. The owner of Synn Citi, who was a business partner of mine, agreed to be a sponsor for the show, but gave me one of the best runarounds I've ever experienced in my life.

Nevertheless, Revardo took the cake. This individual lived pretty well off, but you wouldn't know it if you caught him in public; he dressed like an average man to disguise his status. I was introduced to Revardo by an ally of mine since he was in the outdoor events business for 13 years and I could land some advice or funds if need be. He used to organize the Caribbean Festivals all across Florida, but mainly in Miami. He was from Trinidad and had a gorgeous wife from Haiti who was a former supermodel. When I was invited to his home to discuss business, I had to try my hardest not to look at his wife because she had on this white, skintight body suit.

That night, we went over what we had spent, how much more we needed to spend, and what was left to be done. This dude gave us the whole song and dance on how he was going to give us a '05 Escalade for a couple of days as a promotional vehicle, give us his hotel hook-ups, and $3,000 back up money. We didn't ask for all of this, but he felt that we needed the assistance. He was promising too many things to us and that was a red flag for me. In return, we were going to work with him as partners at his soon-to-be club. At the time, I believed him because he had a nice house with two foreign cars plus a

Birth of an Entrepreneur

2006 Navigator. And, he had keys to a new building that was supposed to be his new club. This character did not produce a thing.

Luckily for us, I insisted on having a plan B for everything that he was going to assist us with like the hotel and the limousine. Everything sounded too good to be true, so I put the limousine and hotel on my debit card so I could cancel the transaction just in case Revardo came through. Smart, huh?

Hustling was my first, last, and middle name. I was determined to make the show happen and I needed sponsors worse than Leon Spinks needed teeth. Why use my money when I could use other people's money? Businesses that sponsored the event would get advertisement in exchange, the costs of the event are underwritten, and then, I get paid – it was an even exchange. I even stepped to my traffic ticket attorney, but she turned me down. Her staff called a number on a sample flyer that I had given to them. The firm ended up calling one of the rap duo guys that were formerly part of the team, and they cursed the attorney out. They did it so the firm would think it was me who cursed them out. How did this come to my attention? A letter, along with a check came in the mail containing a statement from the firm stating they were going to withdraw from one of the traffic cases.

Sharks are never that nice, but when one of the clerks explained that they were threatened by a person from the number on the flyer I had given them, I realized the duo was behind this. Since the numbers of both Pretty Boy and West

The Courage To Believe

were on the flyer, one of them was on the profane end of the phone. The firm and I ended up smoothing things out once I was able to explain my innocence.

Investors were just as hard to come by as sponsors, but they weren't impossible to get. Dorothy, a black woman who did pretty well for herself in the real estate business came through. Dorothy and I had done business before because it was her strippers that danced at the hotel "Off Probation Bash." She was a bisexual pimp with a green finger. Money made her horny and that's the only way a man could have a chance with her. Things went a little sour between us because a couple hundred dollars was stolen from one of the dancer's purse. Even though I didn't have to, I gave Dorothy $150 to make things smooth between us because I did feel partly responsible. Mainly, I pursued business advice from ambitious people like her. Gifts are necessary to build and restore relationships with influential individuals according to the 48 Laws of Power by Robert Green. We hooked up again at a restaurant while discussing my project. She seemed excited in person, but a couple of days later she reneged. It felt good making moves like that, even though things didn't go my way six out of ten times.

Ticket sales were going pretty good, but we weren't selling them fast enough to get to our goal of $5,000 before prime time. My face was clean on the streets, but there wasn't any dope boy or business associate willing to invest in the project. After some hard thinking, I remembered that once in the past, I forgot my money to buy some high school football playoff tickets. That's when my cousin's friend, Pete, let me borrow $40. The funny thing is, I left my apartment that day for the sole purpose of buying those game tickets, but I left the money on my bed. I repaid him later that night, and that's partially why he trusted me. Pete saved my life whether he realized it or not. Out of all the people that I've done business with or knew personally, Pete was the only one that believed in my vision enough to back me up with stacks of cash ($5,000). I only knew him for about two years. The agreement was 50 percent on his return of the investment totaling $7,500.

In the meantime, "Champagne Thursdays" was going down the drain. On the stage, it looked as if I was neglecting to promote the strip club, but behind the scenes it was the business relationship that deteriorated to the point that my partner wouldn't even show up. He still expected me to pay him his cut. He wanted part of the B.G. show, but I turned him down simply because I neither trusted him nor his judgment. The dancers and the club managers expressed their frustrations to me and there were plenty of remarks about my deal with another club, Club Joseph's. Yes, I could've brought the show to Synn Citi and they would've loved it. However, it could only hold about 200 people. It was obvious that it was only a matter of time until our "Champagne Thursdays" was over.

Watching my Thursdays go from the happening spot to a ghost club was difficult to accept, but he wasn't going to let it go and I wasn't either—not without a fight. The club owner got in the middle and took Thursdays away from both of us because the bottom-line was that the bar wasn't meeting its quota. The

The Courage To Believe

contract was a verbal one that allowed them to terminate their partnership with us. If anything was learned from the strip club, it was that whenever there's a bar there's a millionaire behind the whole operation.

The club tried to throw some extra fees at us within a week of the party. These fees were about $500 dollars, but we never signed the new contract. I was so excited that I would go over to the venue once a week during the daytime when it was open as a restaurant serving lunch. The manager of the club had way too much access to me. He told us one day after a meeting to take down his number, which was a series of sixes -- D.C. looked at me with a look of fear and softly laughed. The rest I don't remember, but after those first three sixes, I wasn't trying to stick it in my memory. Something was dark about his persona and he always dressed in dark, tacky clothes with penny loafers. We needed one last meeting with the owner before the big bash.

May 7th finally came around. I could barely sleep because of all the money we anticipated to make. I was ready to stop driving around in my hooptie (a 1994 white Grand Am Coupe), give Mom a couple of dollars to pay her mortgage, break off my comrades with some money and move out of my brother's apartment. All these dreams were supposed to happen, but not quite…

The block party was supposed to set the tone for the night and B.G. was going to make a surprise appearance at the park. The city commissioners of Pompano Beach had other plans.

They had 20 uniformed officers blocking off the park and sitting under the pavilions. I regret not taking pictures of the officers to use as evidence in a future lawsuit, just in case something jumped off that they would instigate. The police were like kryptonite. They completely shut the park down with their presence. Not to mention that this party was the talk in every ghetto queen, king, and hustler's mouth.

We quickly set up a D.J. one mile away in my old neighborhood. The party wasn't as big as it was supposed to turnout because of the sudden move and understandable confusion. People were dressed in new outfits and brought out their rimmed up cars taking advantage of the opportunity to get their shine on. I knew that this was going to happen, but with all the responsibilities I personally had to handle, there was no choice but to allow the associates in charge of the block party to run it.

A couple of nights prior, I was told by an associate who works at a commissioner's office that the city had an emergency meeting and my block party was the topic du jour. Since I wasn't notified, no one from my side was there to speak on our behalf. According to my inside dude who worked in city hall, Dante Colesto, cops couldn't wait for Sunday, May 7th to come around so that they could harass us. The city commissioners gave the police the green light; politics at their finest. Yup, good ol' South Florida where on Memorial Day 2011, a block party at South Beach made national news when police shot and killed a driver, shot and injured innocent bystanders, "allegedly" took the cell phones of witnesses and smashed them in an effort to try to stop video images from surfacing, and even confiscated the camera of a local news program. Did I mention that just about all of the party-goers were black folk? CNN still aired some of the footage of police robbing a phone at gunpoint. Thanks to quick thinking, a guy managed to slip the memory card into his mouth before the officer threw the phone forcefully to the ground.

We had the entire park rented May 7, 2006 along with permission from the neighboring businesses to use their parking lots. What we didn't have was a permit and that's where they got us. Dante told me if I could get some strippers for him and some of his local, political friends that they would call the dogs off. The dancers came a dime a dozen to me so it was nothing to make that happen. But, I remember feeling like I was in a movie getting bribed by the two-bit crony fronting like the boss man, who wasn't actually as big as he claimed. Not to my surprise, he was full of it. The shame of it was that it was a beautiful, sunny day with a cool breeze; perfect outdoors weather.

Nighttime rolled around and it was on and poppin'. Guess what? Another trick was pulled out the proverbial hat. Fort Lauderdale police and the security company that was hired wanted $1,000 each before the doors of the club opened. We were in the ocean and the sharks smelled blood. The audacity of these people was unbelievable! Everybody was in our pockets. Everybody! Snakes came from under every rock. That Biggie Smalls song saying, "Mo' Money - More Problems," couldn't have been said any better.

Birth of an Entrepreneur

They had us by our throats for a second, but they underestimated us as businessmen. I guess they had to try; however, we were able to come to an understanding with them that by midnight, a payment would be made. The officer in charge even gave a speech warning officers to look out for the Haitians, "They are vicious animals that will get into fights, go into the trunks of their cars to hunt and kill with Ak-47s." On the other hand, Tony, B.G.'s manager, gave us back the $2,000 once he saw the flyer for himself and realized the flyer never stated his artist would be at Apollo Park. That was totally unexpected, but thanks to the slick talk of D.C., the whole ordeal was water under the bridge.

That night, I felt like somebody important. I always had that demeanor about myself, but now I had something else to show for it. I was dressed in a black, long sleeved shirt, with black, Armani pants, and black, Gucci shoes. A line formed outside before the club was even open; every promoter's dream as a result of hard work on behalf of everyone who played their role in promoting the event. We packed the club, but it was nothing like the Easter night event. The great fiasco of the Easter bash was that all the money made at the entrance of the PSC show was collected by the duo and stolen by a third partner of theirs—an estimated $40,000.

Pharo and the rest of the Dollarz and Centz squad performed like they were the headliner of the show. Pharo had not yet been out of jail for a month and was enjoying every moment on stage. It felt good watching him do what he loves to do, which is being the center of attention, talking jazz.

The Courage To Believe

Dollarz and Centz performed five songs, but they were only scheduled to do two.

Next, B.G. hit the stage and the crowd went bananas. He really knows how to work the audience. There were a lot of pictures taken with his fans and he autographed a poster for my Goddaughter, Rachael. I didn't take a picture or get on camera with him; we just exchanged a word or two and kept it moving. He's a G and I'm a G...no groupie over here. I am, however, a fan of his music, his struggle with the street life, and his determined drug addiction battle. He performed for 30 minutes when he only had to be on stage for 12 minutes according to the contract.

Fights erupted throughout the crowd, so we disappeared to count our cash in a fancy hotel across town. The moment we have been waiting for—we counted a little over $10,000. My mouth dropped in disappointment, even though that was the most money that I've ever counted with my hands. We counted the money again and there wasn't a big difference. All I can remember saying in my head was **$10,000; $10,000; $10,000!?!** In actuality, we made $29,000, but spent $19,000 in total once adding the ticket sales and the amount we paid the pigs. D.C. and I split it 50/50, $5,000 each.

Two things happened to me after that night: 1) One Man Army, Inc. became very popular locally, and 2) I went broke, believe it or not. The latter wasn't in the game plan. The next morning I gave Pete every dollar that was put into my hands: $5,035. All that work and I didn't walk out with five bucks to put gas in my car—seriously. The state of depression was so severe that it caused me to not even think about compensating myself for the work I put in before paying my friend back. I am a man of my word, so whenever I say I'm going to do something—no matter what it is—I do it, especially if someone's depending on me to come through. When it comes to belongings that are borrowed or stolen from us, whether it be money, a book, a car, or whatever, that which was stolen must be returned to the owner or else negative energy will be drawn between both sides. I had a little stash, but that also quickly vanished.

I made many crucial mistakes. I put too much of me into that project. That's typical Kevin Dorival; whenever I put my heart into something, I go all out. Mentally, physically, and financially, I lost by producing that show and got nothing in return. The number one rule in business is to profit as much as possible. A lot of people felt I was on top of the world or was about to be there.

My family began to ask for money that wasn't there and some of them thought I was lying. To make matters worse, my bank made a mistake depositing $1,500 cash into my personal checking instead of my business account. The check that I wrote two weeks prior to the club had bounced because of this mistake. They were blowing my phone up for the money and mentioned that charges would be pressed. In order to buy myself time, I told them that I was in New York in the middle of an internship and wouldn't be back until June 2nd. I was selling crack, so coming up with the money wouldn't be as hard

The Courage To Believe

as it would've been if I were working a 9 to 5 gig; I was working the flip side…9:00 p.m. to 5:00 a.m., the vampire shift. Ever since the last show, I had been in debt. It was as if a financial spell was put on me or something.

I was taking hits from left and right with street debts and bills. The street debts were paid-in-full for the most part. They had to take cutbacks on the interest that was promised. Because of that show, I lost D.C. as a friend and a business partner. Money brought us together and money tore us apart. He lied to me and took the $2,000 that the artist's manager returned to us. It's a shame, because we were a great team with two totally different styles that complimented each other's talents.

I took the little money that I had in the bank, which was about $700, and bought as much dope as I could. One by one, most of the student loans, banking fees, and lenders were all paid…slowly. All I had to do was sell crack. Yeah, I went the street route, but of all the commodities with fail proof customers, crack users return 100 percent of the time until they either get that monkey off their back, or it chokes them to death. It took a lot for me to accept the reality that I had to degrade myself to make ends meet. This isn't what I went into exile, graduated college, and slept in my car to do. There was more to life than chasing money and fast girls. I was now more interested in the simpler things in life like smelling the roses and listening to the ocean roar under a sparkling, moonlit sky.

TWENTY

I Have a Dream

On September 7, 2007, I was part of an important march in Jena, Louisiana. "Jena 6" was quite an experience and one that I shall proudly carry with me for the rest of my life. Taking this 34-hour road trip (17 hour drive both ways) with about 40 other dedicated activists that felt like they had to "Get on the Bus" taught me the meaning of unity and most importantly, the power of people in synergy to effect change. I took part in the march because of the injustice that continues to plague our democratic land in this 21st century. The audacity of the authorities to charge these six young males with attempted murder for a school fight that was started by other individuals was baffling to me and absurd.

The Louisiana weather was perfect with a nice, cool breeze and radiant sun shining on our beautiful skin that Thursday afternoon. "No Justice - No Peace," was shouted uniformly by the thousands. We had something to prove, something to stand for - all 15,000 of us. Al Sharpton, Michael Baisden, and many of the Louisiana State University (LSU) students were amongst the protestors. All the businesses surrounding the school of the attacks of the white students, allegedly perpetrated by blacks, were shut down because they were afraid a riot would erupt. They lost out on a lot of business because we had money and wanted to buy things like water or food. Every store would have made their quota for the

The Courage To Believe

year had they been open that day. Surprising to me, some of the shops had signs up stating, "We don't serve blacks." Wow! It's 2007 and those signs were a slap in the face to any individual who thought we lived in the post-civil rights era. We are supposed to be moving forward as a nation and leave the past behind, but it seems history will always repeat itself somehow, someway. Dr. Martin Luther King, Jr. marched against the same racial ignorance 45 years ago during his era. My eyes got watery while others broke down and cried once we stepped off the bus and realized that our people marched for the same reasons in the 1960's, but they were met by brutality from the police. This had to take some courage knowing that they would get beat down.

Dr. Martin Luther King was a visionary. What we are seeing in this new millennium is what Dr. King envisioned a long time ago: people loving each other, working, walking, and eating together equally.

> Where would America be if Dr. King never existed?

Dr. King is on the same level as Jesus Christ as far as the legacy of biblical importance, by sacrificing their lives for the better of the human race. Where would America be if Dr. King never existed?

Unfortunately, many people work on Dr. Martin Luther King Day, and I'm sure he would have understood because for the most part, if we don't work, we don't eat. But, do many of us really have to work on January 15th year after year? It really is a pity that the gravity of the legacy of Dr. King's extraordinarily life continues to escape most of us. I like that President Obama is trying to re-inject meaning into MLK Day by encouraging Americans to serve their communities in some way to reflect the way Dr. King served the entire country, for what he did was not just for black folks, but for the betterment of the nation and the world. I truly appreciate that his birthday is still a legacy that hasn't faded away in most regions. As a child, I can recall saying to myself that I wasn't black because of my light brown complexion. When every social reference around us places all things black as negative—black cats, black magic, even devil's food cake being dark chocolate—it's only natural that a child would shy away from being "black". There was a constant social imprinting that black equaled bad, wrong, and just plain evil. There's a disconnect between knowing there's nothing wrong with oneself inside of one's black skin and the fact that bad guys wear black.

Even in the primary school reader, the black puppy is the mischievous one and the white one is angelic. Eventually, a light bulb went off in my head and I began feeling proud that I was black. Many times the classic James Brown song, "I'm Black and I'm proud" played in my head. It's a very famous song, but most people aren't aware of the controversy and the heat that Mr. Brown took on as a result of the release of that song, even from other prominent African Americans. The Black Panthers loved it because of the strong message it sent out to black children and adults: "Say it loud, I'm black and I'm proud." The timing was perfect for the 70's. It was near the beginning of the revolution…around the time when we started to become united as a nation.

The Courage To Believe

It takes a powerful person to be committed to non-violent protesting, especially when everything around Martin L. King, Jr. movement was violent. He was a pure genius! Fight back your adversary with positive energy. Attack hate with love, violence with peace, hunger with food, and ignorance with knowledge. Today's generation could learn a lot from the past like how to fight STD's with abstinence. The rates of black on black violence in today's society are so alarming that it would I'm sure Dr. King is turning in his grave.

In 2002, African Americans were 12% of the United States population, yet 47% of all homicide victims. The first week of January 2007 was the week before MLK Day. In Miami, a mother, her son, and his girlfriend were all gunned down in a car leaving only the mother barely surviving. These fatal incidents happen all the time due to the misguided energy of frustrated black males. The black on black crime epidemic has been going on for a very long time, and it stems from the roots of injustice starting from the birth of America. Since 1980, there have been approximately 325,000 deaths of black men at the hands of black offenders. Current statistics also show that approximately 38% of the black males in America are either in prison, on probation or on parole.

I posed this question, "Has the value of life depreciated as the perceived value of material things increased?" What does family mean today to our society? Does it even matter that we all bleed the same color and that we all—all of us come from the motherland of Africa? Does it even matter that we are all members of the human race? In terms of our race, our genes, and our species, we are Homo sapiens. It really is antiquated terminology people use when we ignore what we learned in biology class about the species and continue to define our differences of skin color in terms of "race." Homo sapiens and Simians are truly different races of creatures, so the trouble with people carrying racial definitions of each other from slave days into the new millennium is that it encourages one so-called race to think of themselves higher on the evolutionary chain than the other so-called races. Racism. When we fill out government forms and are asked to check our race, the choices presented are different ethnicities, cultures, and skin colors, yet all are still the solitary human race.

The idea of "race" is something humans added to the description of Homo sapiens and because we've been so conditioned all our lives, we all participate in perpetuating the misinformed, unscientific lie; a lie likely created to conjure up the image of that evolution chart showing an ape slowly morphing into an upright walking man. From there, people are supposed to presume that ethnicities other than white are less evolved than the last image of upright man. Science tells us that Homo Sapien means "man who thinks." So, we are all equals as well as all of those with African descent, as proved by the Human Genome Project (The National Human Genome Research Institute).

Our differences should be celebrated as the colorful kaleidoscope of humanity God has created. Instead, the outdated and inaccurate language of racism makes those who think of themselves as the superior so-called race denigrate others rather than venerate them. If we all would begin daily to replace that one, little word, "race" with the proper term "ethnicity," would it make a difference in reframing our world? Would changing our speech begin to change our thinking? Rather than continue to follow the lead of those who proclaimed themselves higher beings, perhaps we should act upon what we know to be true and replace that word "race" with "ethnicity, color, or culture." Though African Americans have come a long way, unless we begin speaking truth, black and brown people will always be second-class citizens. It will take daily discipline, but all meaningful change that makes the world a better place requires love, courage, and patience.

I'm proud of my African heritage as well as my Haitian cultural roots. It just gets me sick to my stomach sometimes when I see the direction African Americans are heading. We've come so far from being the outcasts of a society that upheld a hypocritical constitution through decades and even worse, centuries. I appreciate what my brothers and sisters of yesteryear did for me with the sit-ins, boycotts, and marches during the 1960's. It took a lot of courage from the Student Non-violent Coordinating Committee (SNCC) to sit in diners across the country knowing they would get struck and spit on. It took amazing discipline to carpool with strangers and walk miles to work due to the lack of respect the transit system had for black people. This happened to be the main source of income for the buses in the first place.

I have not forgotten what they have done for me and my future children; my grandchildren won't forget the struggle behind our freedom. I thank you revolutionary souljas. I spell soldiers spelled with soul; "Souljas," because you can protect life or take life very easily, but it benefits our community when a person takes the time to touch a person's soul, whether it is through an act of kindness or with encouragement. That act of kindness is a blessing that will be given to someone else and in return, that person will give it to another, and so on, and so forth. We can call it a "Cycle of Blessings or Pay It Forward."

In the United States of America, we have currently been taking regressive steps from what the Civil Rights Movement originally represented. We began with fighting to get equal rights for everyone collectively, no matter what color or gender you were. Now we just worry about ourselves or about those that can increase our wealth or status. There is so much ignorance and lack of knowledge in many black communities that it's unbearable to even imagine what the future holds for us. Maybe selfishness is just a South Florida thing because I've been told that in Jacksonville, Atlanta, D.C., Baltimore and Chicago, the black communities are well grounded by supporting each other. One hand washes the other is the way it should be.

The ignorance in our communities has caused me to use two words wisely and I don't use them loosely: family and home. Everything starts at home and the dilemma we face today is that there are far too many houses rather than homes. My generation, Generation X, is filled with homeless women and men. Just because you pay a mortgage on a property doesn't mean that it's a home. A house to someone could be a cardboard box, but as long as they have peace of mind being in that cardboard box, then they have the right to call it their home. "Home is where the heart is" as the proverb says. There's not enough love where we lay our heads. If there's no love in our houses, then why would we care about our neighborhood or our country? It's a domino effect. Parents sleeping under different roofs cause the child to only learn from one world instead of two. Sisters and brothers don't even know of each other's whereabouts or even care about how their siblings are living or eating. This behavior dismantles the natural order of any family and should be put to cease.

I want a woman I can grow and learn with because dealing with someone like me, she will definitely learn quite a bit. If I can't treat my woman like a queen, then it really isn't too interesting. Being romantic with candles, writing thoughtful notes and letters that show her she's the center of my world is something that has been difficult for me because I was in the trenches for so long. I found it difficult to be a Casanova while I was Saving Private Ryan, but I'm growing and learning from this perspective.

. . . .

Meanwhile, I was trying to save my youngest brother Pharo, who was always ambitious, outspoken and outgoing. When he was in elementary school, the doctors put him on medication to slow down his behavior due to his hyper personality. These pills would make him sleep constantly, but they kept him from fights that he would partake in as if they were his daily ritual. Needless to say, he was taken off those pills, and over the years, he got into a lot of trouble with the law. Pharo developed a bad reputation on the streets and amongst the police by the time he was 15 years old. He was an Amtrak Train with no brakes heading nowhere fast. Eventually, he would have his first child at the age of 20 and his second at the age of 22; needless to say, two adorable young men. Unfortunately, Pharo never got a chance to see them born because he would always be in the county jail fighting for his life and our gracious God would give him victory after victory.

Drunk with confidence, he continued to run the streets maliciously. I made it my business to show him what I was trying to do with my clothing line and make it a family business like Master P (Percy Miller) did with No Limit. Out of all my brothers, he was the biggest help in pushing my T-shirts on the streets. He even went with me to a few events where I had a table as a vendor selling the OMA shirts displayed. Something was boiling inside of him because I never could get through to him - no one could. In 2006, he beat an attempted murder case. While he was locked up, the alleged victim was shot down. His death was blamed on my brother's friends...members of a group called "Doom City Boyz (DCB)." Doom City Boyz were in the newspaper and television on a regular basis. If you were a Haitian male and lived in Deerfield Beach, the police labeled you as a gang member from the DCB group. They were banned from many locales like schools and clubs. Nine members of the group are serving life sentences in Florida state prisons. Several of them are serving time in federal prisons scattered across the county. My brother Pharo had a great lawyer, Matthew Couglas, who fought like a pit-bull in the courtroom; Pharo needed one, since they believed he was the leader of the DCB. After the acquittal, we celebrated with Matthew at Synn City, the strip club that I had hosted every Thursday night.

The Courage To Believe

Unfortunately, months after his victory, our mother was diagnosed with cancer in her spine (Multiple Myeloma). All of her children took this hard. You never perceive that something like cancer can happen to you or your family until it happens. My world came crashing down instantly. She was everything to me and it greatly depressed me to know she was suffering and I couldn't do anything about it. By this time, Pharo straight lost it. Instead of using his pain to propel him towards his goals, he used it to inject pain on others. A year after he won his case, he was placed in the fire again when he allegedly was involved in a robbery with three of friends of a drug dealer that one of which happened to be a police informant. By the time the robbery was over, one person got killed in a high-speed chase from the police. My brother and his friends were sentenced to life in prison due to this death. I wish I could have done more to save my brother from his reckless ways, especially after I had two strange dreams.

The first dream was about me buying a Blue Cadillac Escalade with 22-inch rims off of the showroom floor in a Fort Lauderdale dealership. I drove the SUV right to my grandma's house to show off the truck to my brothers. I got there as the sun was setting. Police rushed the house, arresting one of my brothers, but I'm not sure which one. I could only think that this sign meant God was telling me I was going to be blessed, but one of my brothers would be taken away—quid pro quo.

One week later, I had another dramatic dream. I'm sleeping in my dark room and I'm awakened by the stream of sunlight from my door. As a got up, I saw an M-16. I jumped up out of my bed; grabbed one of my swords that were hanging forming an X over my headboard. I swung the sword upward hitting the rifle towards the ceiling as the assailant creeps in. Next, I ran out my room only to meet more masked men. All of them pointed their guns directly at my head and began shooting rapidly. I woke up in a cold sweat gasping for air and thanking God that this was only a nightmare.

The latter dream was more dramatic than the first one. I knew that God was giving me a sign due to the fact that the last time I was given a similar dream someone died. So, I warned my brothers about the dreams and advise them to stop whatever illegal activities they were doing because something of grave danger is about to happen. I stressed to my little brother Pharo to cease his illegal activities because I heard rumors of his black mailing and extortion schemes. His actions in the streets were ruining my reputation since many people knew we were brothers. I had to make a lot of deliveries with the shirts and was afraid that retaliation of what he was doing would put me in harm's way. We sat down and smoked a couple of joints discussing his situation and our goals for the family. He was under immense pressure from his two baby mothers and my grandmother (who can be extremely obnoxious) about money they needed from him.

His job at Bed, Bath, and Beyond was barely enough to cover his bills and he felt like he needed a heist to catch-up.

"Pharo, you must be able to see beyond where you are right now because the devil wants you to feel frustrated and discouraged enough to make you do something stupid," I told him, "You need positive friends and a great woman by your side to encourage you."

Pharo replied, "It's easy for you to say this because you don't have any kids and you making money with your clothing line."

By this time, the conversation was getting heated. I told him, "The clothing line isn't just for me; it's for all of us. Get your mind off of today and think about where you see yourself 10 years from now. What will you be doing? Do you think God likes what you are doing to these people? You are out there robbing those bustas…man! They got places for people who think and act like you do and it ain't pretty!"

He replied, "I don't give a ^&%$#@ where I end up. I got bills to pay and kids to feed!" Sadly, at that very moment, I realized he was already locked up. My brother was gone.

A few days later, he supposedly robbed a big time dope dealer who happened to work with the police as an informant setting up smaller dealers. Just like the dream showed me, masked men rushing into my grandma's house while I was there is exactly how it happened, except I wasn't in the bed. I was outside getting ready to roll a blunt when I saw a hummer with the S.W.A.T. team hanging on the outside of the vehicle. They passed the house so I felt a brief sense of relief, but then they turned around because they missed the house. I immediately put my hands up and lied down on the hot summer concrete. They were accompanied by some detectives that had search warrants. All the doors were open so they didn't have to kick in any doors except one locked door in the house where my grandpa was sleeping. They handcuffed my grandparents and my mom, who was in a wheelchair at the time. They kept me on the hot pavement lying down on my stomach with no shirt, handcuffed with their foot on my neck, but I never resisted.

They were very disappointed after their search of the house turned up absolutely nothing since we cleaned out the house of any weapons and bullets the same night Pharo got arrested.

One of the cops asked me. "So you are the One Man Army that has been selling all of these shirts we been seeing on the streets?" I replied. "Yes, that's me! Get your foot off my neck man I'm not resisting!"

My older brother J.C. was allegedly involved in a shootout against the victim's family of the robbery and that's why they were there.

"I arrested J.C. earlier today on his way to work," says the detective.

Had I any control over my temper, the conversation I had with Pharo that sunny afternoon would've been received by him. Any person that lives and makes all their decisions based off of their emotions is living a dangerous life. Emotions can cause you to make horrible, rash, unintelligent decisions. I've prayed and practiced for two years that I would not allow my emotions to control me any longer … getting mad just because someone is purposefully trying to make me angry. Cursing back at someone that curses at me was the old Kevin. The new

Kevin is now the Redeemed Kevin and will not allow anyone to drag me into their world of anger, ignorance or negativity. Why give anyone that kind of power over me? I am very convinced that Pharo cursed himself that afternoon by stating that he didn't care where he ended up - dead or prison. He is currently in Okeechobee Correctional Institute fighting to get an appeal on his case. The police and state prosecutors of the city of Pompano, Deerfield, and Fort Lauderdale wanted to stick a murder charge on him and his supposedly Doom City Boyz for years and they finally were victorious this time around, it seemed. God will prevail. It was a shady trial with no witnesses, so an appeal trial is eminent.

My mother was deceased on Memorial Day, May 28, 2008 at 6:15 p.m. Earlier that afternoon, J.C. and I were at the hospital with her and her last words to us were:

"Don't forget the bible."

Everything else was mumbled and hard to make out. It was tough seeing her in the state that she was in. She died before the conclusion of Pharo's case.

Making the arrangements for her funeral was new to us. How do you prepare to lay your mother, our Queen, to rest? I never cried during the funeral, just numb. My tears were shed the days prior and days after. It was a great honor to carry her casket down the aisle into the hearse with J.C., Uncle Joe, and Uncle Eugene (her two brothers). Our family and family friends came to support us. Over the years I've known plenty of people that lost their moms much too early. Now I know and painfully understand how it feels. We all took her home-going as motivation to continue what she expected of us which was to take care of her grandbabies and succeed in life. "Life is hard. Do your best to avoid a hard life," my mom would always tell us and I will forever remember that. I am privileged to be her son due to the fact we all know there aren't too many honorable people left in the world.

TWENTY-ONE

A New Leaf

If there is any particular message that I would like you to take hold of from my life, it's to hang in there no matter the circumstance. Quitting is not an option when you were created to be Victorious. Always speak positive so you can think positive. You can curse yourself and others with your words, but you can also bless yourself by the choice of words you use and the thoughts on which you dwell. The latter is preferred for obvious reasons ... the more positive your thinking, the more positive your words, and ultimately, the more positive your world. Even when the odds are against you in achieving your goals, or you find yourself in a situation that appears to be getting worse instead of better, always remain positive. Smile in the face of adversity; rejoicing when others may cry.

It is a matter of what or who you're giving credit to; what are you magnifying? Are you feeding your problems or are you feeding your dreams? One will strive and the other will starve. You feed and magnify them by the words you speak. In Proverbs 18:21 (NIV), it says, "The tongue has the power of life and death and those who love it will eat its fruit." I didn't grasp that scripture at first, but it didn't take long before I became a doer and began to speak the Word over every obstacle that showed up in my life, especially since I expected to produce fruit good enough to eat. If you continue to feed your problems with fear and doubt, they will mature into depression, isolation and hopelessness, just to name a few.

Regardless of your age, always know your successes or failures are predestined. Now, that doesn't mean that effort, hard work and will power aren't required. It's just that there is a divine plan that goes beyond your natural plan to that of The Master's Plan for your life. In other words, no matter how far we may stray off the path, which leads directly to our purpose and destiny, God will always use mistakes we make in life for our good and his glory. He cares more than we do that we hit the mark for which we were created. There are times when his answer to our prayer may be a resounding

"No." Keep in mind, Father knows best and his "No" at that time is in our best interest.

"No, you only see a shiny apple, but I know the dangers unseen within that apple."

"No, not yet, because I am still working bad habits and attitudes out of you; character – development."

"No," could further mean, "If I gave you the million now, it would be gone in six months from lack of financial maturity?"

Everything concerning you has been written, pre-ordained for your life, you just have to speak it into existence, and of course, get off your butt of doing nothing and make the necessary changes. Get in position and stop making excuses for what you meant to do! Believe it or not, but "procrastination" is a curse. Each of us have an inner power deep within to rise and shine, but subconsciously for some of us, it's been lethargically dormant due to the hot flames of adversity.

My regular prayer is that the Lord waves his hands to clear my path of weapons, enemies, and mountains that seem to pop up every time I'm working towards achieving greatness. I am a living witness that prayer works and it will keep you synchronized with his will for your life.

There were countless times when I didn't know how or even if I would survive the oppositions placed before me. I would ask myself, "*Could a happy ending be possible?"* When my brothers and sisters were taken away by HRS (Human Rehabilitative Services), when the authorities swarmed our home without a warrant, when I was locked up in between classes and legal battles abound, when I was viciously attacked by dogs, waking up at 4:00a.m - to catch buses and trains (Lord knows I am not a morning person) to go to school crossing three counties, etc… With all that drama, it was the prayers that were prayed on my behalf by family and close allies that saved me and gave me motivation to press on.

One Man Army represents — one man, one soldier in heaven's army, a determined entrepreneur under a name that is a metaphor for ambition. Any single mother, father, student, soldier, inmate, teacher, attorney, doctor, nurse, businessperson or artist can look at themselves as a One Woman Army and One Man Army. However, no one is an island and as my Apostle, Yvette Brinson, always says: "that's stinking thinking."

A New Leaf

We were created to coexist with others and our social skills were introduced as early as kindergarten. Think about it. The activities and games we were first taught, usually called for a team or teams which aided in our social development and thereby forming friendships that would last for a reason, a season or even a lifetime. Even though I still have a handful of friends from kindergarten, I am thankful for my early social interaction. But given the choice back then to play by myself, surely I would have chosen solitude.

My thinking as early as kindergarten was that I only needed 'me, myself and I' to fulfill my dreams, my goals, my purpose in life. That "stinking thinking" behavior was carried over into adulthood and it manifested in me coining myself as a One Man Army because I found it hard to find trust worthy people.

It wasn't until I created my marketing company under the name One Man Army, Inc., that the light-bulb suddenly came on. It happened, as a matter of fact, when my clients were more focused on the meaning behind the name of the company than the marketing services being offered. Change had to happen and it had to happen quickly with speed and depth. Hence, the name One Man Army, Inc. was buried and "Sky View Marketing" was erected. That's a great example of thinking outside the box... "Going Beyond!" The phrase "no one is an island" is more than just mere words, its veracity, its truth. The more energy I spent reading, hearing and spending time with the author of truth, the more my old mind-set, my old way of thinking began to change. A transformation began and I enjoyed the inner peace even though my surroundings were upside down. The Bible says:

"Do not conform to the pattern of this world, but be transformed by the renewing of your mind. Then you will be able to test and approve what God's will is —his good, pleasing and perfect will. For by the grace given me I say to every one of you: Do not think of yourself more highly than you ought, but rather think of yourself with sober judgment, in accordance with the faith God has distributed to each of you. Romans 12:2-3 (NIV).

In other words, at some point in life, we will need the encouragement, assistance and prayers of others. Don't let the problems of your world change what makes you beautiful as a person. Now that my mind has been renewed and transformed by the Word of God (the author of Truth), my vision went from seeing through solitary lenses (my eyes only) to seeing through the eyes of my creator – from the perception of a Sky View. Was my thinking too small, even though I had big dreams? Did I really have "The Courage to Believe" that I could be successful, and make a difference in this world?

I was finally making the right choices and my vision was aligning with his will, his way of doing, seeing, breathing and living. My belief level is high and I am ready to fulfill my purpose and destiny. The greater the call or purpose that's on your life, the greater the enemy you will likely have to contend with. Be patient, strategize and you will have the victory!

In doing this, I hope to become your reward as I challenge you to accomplish what has been prophesied over your life. I am more determined than ever to make a difference in the world by starting with "the man in the mirror." But it began with me having the courage to believe in my blessings of knowledge, wisdom and understanding. Believe in God, who is the author and finisher of your vision. Believe in yourself, that without him, you can do nothing, but with him, you can do all things. Take the time to fellowship with the Lord, by spending time in the good book and his presence — you will increase in strength both physically and spiritually. There will be times when your physical strength won't be enough to sustain you, but your spirit will give you that push to move mountains by faith . . .to move forward.

Generation X, my generation, bred an era of hungry individuals, but the reality is that it's in our DNA to be creative, successful business owners, trend setters, and most importantly, survivors. Like me, you may have a prior felony record and feel that you are a second-class citizen, but don't believe the hype! Refuse to accept that branding from the system. The pain and struggle of hanging in there day after day comes with the territory, despite getting doors closed in your face because of your past mistakes. Never give up! Some of the greatest followers of Christ in the bible had a soiled history until God through the Son, stepped in.

Are you ready to embrace change and become who God says you are? Do you have the Courage to Persevere? Look at all the technology around us: tablets, smart phones, talking cars, social media sites, and the rise of online businesses. You can create your future by putting God first, sowing good seeds and putting action behind your faith (The best recipe for success.)

The Courage To Believe

This very book didn't manifest without opposition of every kind. You name it, I have been there and back again with all the difficulties of getting it published and making it available to the public. I never gave up! There may be employment opportunities lost for whatever reason. Never give up! As soon as a little money flows in, something comes up and it goes right back out. Never give up! Instead just rejoice at the devil for trying to attack your finances. His army of darkness is a defeated foe.

My aspiration to break my family's curse has finally manifested and the proof is in the pudding. For years I've been planting positive seeds into my life and into the lives of the majority of the people I've met. I had a dream, wrote it down on paper, spoke it into existence, and did everything in my power to see it through with the right people on my side. It doesn't matter whether you enter from the front door or the back door, just get across the threshold or, assist someone else with a desire to "Go Beyond" with the right motive in their heart. Become an answer and help mold our society with your efforts ... good intentions can open doors of success, and, in this way, we'll help mold society into a better place. One never knows when positive deeds may have prevented someone from destruction by selling their body or committing suicide.

We were made to be interdependent; first on God and then on each other. One is too small of a number to achieve great success. As a young boy, I craved for the love of my biological father, but I'm thankful for my mother who showed us the value of work, love and faith.

A New Leaf

Like many of us I magnified the negative things instead of the positive and got into big trouble. I was caught up in trying to pay the massive amounts of bills that were piling up by the day: rent, student loans, and credit cards... only in America. After every deal, whether it was from my suppliers or the ones I supplied, I felt like I was losing a piece of my soul. But, the finality of my illegal activities transpired once my hunger to draw closer to God intensified. Life pretty much fell into perspective as I pressed in to remain synchronized with his will for my life.

I decided to no longer place my freedom in jeopardy because I knew that it was worth a lot more in the future—perhaps billions. Being behind closed walls and bars wasn't made for us and definitely not for his blessed children ... not for a king or a queen. I always felt that God was telling me if I ceased eating from the devils table, he would bless whatever I put my hands to in order to expand his kingdom as well as a good life for my future wife and kids. For the first time in my life, I began to feel confident of my purpose on earth. My life began to have a meaning, a purpose of great magnitude that will have an impact on the world in a positive way. The coin wasn't going to flip ever again. We each have a calling in this life ... something to build upon or to add on for the advancement of our next generation, our neighbors, and the world.

You've read quite a bit about my life; the puzzling childhood adventures, my adult tribulations, and the victories. I've never tooted my own horn on being a saint because nobody's perfect except the one who guided me in writing this book, my Heavenly Father. God brought me through every trial and tribulation (though most were self-inflected.) to a place where I am free and without shame to turn my life into an open book in order to inspire and prevent you or someone like me to not make the same self-inflicted mistakes which can land you behind bars or below ground. The Bible says that it was the spirit of God that drove certain men, the prophets and apostles, to pen what He told them to put down on paper; I accepted that belief and followed suit. Through my Faith and Trust in God, I have manifested into the man I am today.

It was critical for me to find a church with a leader that I felt was righteous in order for me to honor him or her. Pastor Verna DuPont filled that void at the time. I joined "New Beginnings Christian Center" after a year of visiting on and off. A colleague of mine at FAU, Krystal Hayward, introduced me to New Beginnings after my initial intention was to pursue her in courtship. Even though I didn't apply faith to all aspects of my life, I was claiming that I had faith. I recall seeking guidance and truth on the wrong road, so Krystal took advantage of the situation to invite me to church with her. I will be forever indebted to her for reintroducing me to the light during a dark era in my life.

Who was I kidding thinking that I could deal with this massive world by myself? Sure, anyone can try, but just like a true teacher, Jesus waits patiently for us to turnaround and asks for his help. Today, I honor my bible like I honor family values; that is why there is so much inspiration to keep moving forward no matter what comes my way, even when I don't have the strength to do so.

Preachers are placed in our paths to give us spiritual guidance. After about two years, I left New Beginnings and started a new beginning at Redeeming Word Christian Center International ("RWCCI"), Pastored by Apostles Ed and Yvette Brinson in Fort Lauderdale, Florida.

The main facet of my life that I want readers to cleave to is that your destiny is in your hands. Only you have control of your actions. Leave no rock unturned. Write your dreams down and make it plain. Zig Ziglar, the famous motivational speaker said it best, "A goal properly set is halfway reached. Find out the dream or goal at hand and target it to see that it gets executed to its fullest nature." Remember, do not procrastinate; it's an evil spirit that wants you to be lazy and miss out on your purpose, destiny and ultimate blessings. I am very appreciative that I had made the decision a long time ago to make a U-turn with my life because I was heading toward a dead end. Now, I am not saying that it will be an easy ride to success; everyone would be successful if that was the case. There will be struggles and hurdles along the way, but anything worth having is worth fighting for. Fredrick Douglas, once said, "If there is no struggle, there is no progress." So fight for what you believe in, whether it is for a family, success, or simply peace of mind. Fight for it with everything you got because there will be negative forces that will try and make sure you fail. You won't fail if you are prepared, proactive and prayed up!

If you can see it, believe in it, then it is possible to attain it. There is so much more to life than money and fame. The cure was to change my way of thinking, which became easier to do once I changed my environment, but most of all, once I became in sync with my mind, body and spirit. It's that simple.

Once I realized that material things weren't going to cure me of my obsession to become successful, I stopped thinking like a bastard and started to think clear with a presence of mind as a son of God, a King's kid. Living a life like that would mean the world to me. Lillian Dickson once said, "Life is like a coin. You can spend it any way you wish, but you only spend it once." Which way will you decide to spend your life today? Make the decision now and begin living your life the way it was destined to be! Become one with the Father and get synchronized with His will for your Life.

It's only appropriate to end the story of my life like the history of my parent's country, my country—Haiti; strong, tenacious, and looking toward the future. My life has had two main parts; one that was headed south, and the remainder that is climbing to higher heights. The latter is my hope and the bible says "your latter will be greater." Will yours? Do you have the Courage to Believe?

You have all the tools to be great. Until the next time…God Bless.

The Beginning…

Works Cited

Clark, Ramsey. "Haiti's Agonies and Exaltations." 17 March 2009. The Haitian Bicentennial: Rediscovering Haiti. 5 October 2011 <http://faculty.lagcc.cuny.edu/ctl/haiti/agonies_exaltations.htm>.

Congress, The Library of. "Harriet Tubman." 20 February 2008. About.com Inventors. 22 April 2011 <http://inventors.about.com/library/inventors/blharriettubman.htm>.

Heinl, Nancy & Robert. Written In Blood: The Story Of The Haitian People, 1492-1995. New York: United Press of America, 2005. Pages: 91

Kneib, Martha. Benin: Cultures Of The World. Times Publishing Limited, n.d.

NLT. "Hosea." Foundation, Tyndale House. Holy Bible. Carol Stream: Tyndale House Publishers, 2007. 532.

BSO. Sheriff.org. 11 July 1979. 29 May 2006 <http://sheriff.org/about_bso/other/memoriam/conte/index.cfm>.

Ridgeway, James. The Haiti Files: Decoding The Crisis. D.C.: Essential Books, 1994.

Rogozinski, Jan. A Brief History of the Caribbean: From The Arawak And The Carib To The Present. New York: Penguin Group, 2000. Pages: 171

The Courage To Believe

Available Books & Products Coming Soon/ Services:

- "7 Types of Queens, Kings Desire" - 2015
- Documentary, The Courage To Believe: Never Give Up – 2015
- Stage Play: The Courage To Believe – Available
- Book: The Courage To Believe – Available on iTunes.
- Black On Black Crime Solutions Movement – Donate
- "7 Types of Kings, Queens Desire" - 2016
- Children's book, "King Kevin's Courage" - 2016

I am the president of *The Courage To Believe International*, which is a non-profit organization that provides mentoring, educational, enrichment and scholarship programs for at risk youths and young adults. We serve the South Florida communities between the ages of 12 to 21 years. We provide preventative and intervention programs and services that are designed to successfully create positive changes in the lives of our participants. For bookings, contact us: info@couragetobelievebook.com

Life Skills Workshops/ Lectures:

- ☐ How To Stay Focus While In The Fires Of Life
- ☐ How To Find The King & Queen In You
- ☐ Black Authors That Paved The Way
- ☐ History of the Caribbean
- ☐ Avoid Police Brutality
- ☐ Creating Your Future
- ☐ Black On Black Crime Solutions
- ☐ 10 Ways To Find Courage
- ☐ Getting Your Book Published NOW!

The Courage To Believe

For Speaking, Book Coaching, Marketing Services, or Workshop Inquires Contact me at: Info@couragetobelievebook.com

If you liked the book please let your opinions be heard on book's page on: Amazon.com, BN.com, and GoodReads.com

If you found mistakes in this book or have suggestion or comments, please contact me at: thecouragetobelieve@gmail.com - Subject: Book Errors

Want to be kept up to date with what's going on in my life or for the latest products, sign up for my newsletter: thecouragetobelieve@gmail.com - Subject: Signup

I'm A Cool King – Follow Me On

Social Media:

Facebook: Kevin Dorival. The Courage To Believe Book.
Twitter & Instagram: @Courage2Believe
Google +: Kevin Dorival
Youtube: Kevin Dorival
Black Planet: @Courage2Believe
GoodReads: Courage2Believe
Tumblr: Courage2Believe

The Courage To Believe